Words Of Wisdom To Live By

Alfred Armand Montapert

He gains wisdom in a happy way, who gains it by another's experience.
— *Plautus*

Down through the ages all men have delighted in gems of wisdom, wit and philosophy, proverbs and sayings both profound and pithy, summing up in a few choice words the best of man's experience.

Words of Wisdom to Live By is an encyclopedia of such gems — but it is more. Here is a rich treasury of prescriptions to help you LIVE . . . BE . . . and HAVE . . . the BEST! There is wit here, laughter and joy . . . but the emphasis is on IDEAS TO LIVE BY!

A man's real business is not only to make a living but to make a LIFE. And what better way than to draw on the accumulated wisdom of the ages, the best that has been thought and said about LEARNING . . . LIVING . . . and ACHIEVING! For to become what we are capable of becoming is our great goal in life. As Thomas Edison said, "If we did all the things we are capable of doing, we would literally astound ourselves."

Here is a book to make a part of your life — to refer to again and again! We learn and grow by the experience of others, and in these pages great minds share their experience of life in all its dimensions. They speak to us today to inspire, delight and comfort . . . and above all to help us get the most out of ourselves!

Each reader will find in this book answers to his own special needs. Open it at random and you're sure to find words that will challenge your ideas, stimulate your thinking, and guide your actions . . . and lead you toward the true JOY OF LIVING.

Alphabetically arranged by subject *Words of Wisdom to Live By* lets you dip at once into topics that interest you, sampling the ideas of many great writers and thinkers. The more important the topic, the richer the harvest of wisdom you will reap.

This is a book to cherish all the days of your life as an unfailing source of wisdom and inspiration . . . a book that will brighten each day, as it helps you to develop the attributes that lie within you . . . and become the BEST that you CAN BE!

BOOKS OF VALUE
2458 Chislehurst Drive
Los Angeles, California 90027

BOOKS BY THE SAME AUTHOR:

DISTILLED WISDOM
Thoughts That Successful Men Live By

THE SUPREME PHILOSOPHY OF MAN
The Laws of Life

PERSONAL PLANNING MANUAL
A Roadmap For Your Life

THE WAY TO HAPPINESS
Formulas To A Better and Happier Life

AROUND THE WORLD ON THE QE2
Your Lifetime Dreams Realized

INSPIRATION & MOTIVATION
Ideas For Successful Living

PRAY TO WIN!
A Blueprint For Success

ADDITIONAL COPIES MAY BE ORDERED FROM:

BOOKS OF VALUE
2458 Chislehurst Drive
Los Angeles CA 90027

*"To quote copiously and well requires
taste, judgment and erudition,
a feeling for the beautiful,
an appreciation of the noble, and
a sense of the profound."*

—*Christian N. Bovee*

WORDS OF WISDOM
TO LIVE BY

AN ENCYCLOPEDIA OF WISDOM
IN CONDENSED FORM

Compiled and Edited by

Alfred Armand Montapert

Here is a collection of man's best thinking . . .
the distilled wisdom of the great . . .
about LEARNING, LIVING, and ACHIEVING.
Practical, Real-Life Wisdom that will help you be many times
more effective, productive, successful and happy!

BOOKSofVALUE
2458 CHISLEHURST DR., LOS ANGELES, CA 90027

SOWING THE SEEDS OF WISDOM · INSPIRATION · LOVE · HAPPINESS

200

IDEA
Who supplies another
with a constructive thought
has enriched them forever.

—Alfred Armand Montapert

Library of Congress Cataloging in Publication Data
Montapert, Alfred Armand.
    Words of Wisdom To Live By
    Great Thoughts, Inspiration, Quotations.

Printed in the United States of America by
BOOKS OF VALUE   ISBN# 0-9603174-5-7

PREFACE

THE CHALLENGE OF LIFE for each of us is to BECOME the BEST person we are capable of becoming. In GOODNESS, in LOVE, in KINDNESS, in CHARACTER, in HELPING EACH OTHER, in the GENEROUS QUALITIES, including the indwelling presence of GOD, and all the permanent qualities of the SPIRITUAL SOUL, that we can enjoy throughout the eternal years.

WORDS OF WISDOM TO LIVE BY is dedicated to that goal. This self-help book offers you a priceless liberal education, and it includes vital prescriptions for ENJOYABLE, SUCCESSFUL LIVING. It will stimulate your thinking and help you to be successful in your work, in your study, and in your everyday living. The ageless prescriptions spelled out in these pages will, if followed, help develop your inner qualities, for that is where your real wealth is.

Employ your time in improving yourself by other men's writings so that you shall come easily by what others have labored hard for.   — Socrates

This book was not designed to be another quotation book. It was compiled and written for the express purpose of condensing the BEST thoughts and advice of the GREATEST men and women in history, in the hope that their distilled wisdom will be a guide to inspire you to build a solid bedrock foundation for a better, nobler life. This volume contains some of the most powerful and persuasive utterances of man . . . words that will inspire, help and delight you.

The short sayings of wise and good men are of great value. They are like the dust of gold or the sparkle of the diamond.   — Tolstoy

He that lays down precepts for the governing of our lives and moderating our passions, obliges humanity, not only in the present, but in all future generations.   — Seneca

PREFACE, *CONTINUED*

Throughout the centuries great men have stood out like the beacons of a lighthouse to guide and enrich their fellows. The examples of these men live on through the years; everyone can benefit from the paths they have illuminated toward a better life. No man is great in and of himself; he must touch the lives of other great beings who will inspire him, lift him, and push him forward.

He is a rich man who can avail himself of all men's faculties.
— *Ralph Waldo Emerson*

This book of wise sayings was undertaken in the belief that there was a need for a book of practical, everyday, usable ideas that would help modern man develop his full potential and be the person he is capable of being. If we are to be highly successful in life, we must look backward to learn from the experience of the greatest minds of the past, then apply this wisdom to the greatest fulfillment of our everyday living. The experience of the sages coupled with our own gives us the unbeatable combination to reach our worthy goals.

The wisdom of the wise and the experience of the ages are perpetuated by quotation.
— *Disraeli*

The several thousand powerful quotations in WORDS OF WISDOM TO LIVE BY were written or spoken by more than 1000 outstanding people. I have tried to compile the thoughts that affect the whole man . . . physical, mental and spiritual. The business of living is to build a LIFE, to make a good life. To make a living is secondary. The man we ought to be shames the man that we are. We must fill our niche. We know that only we must fill it, or it will not be filled.

The aim of every man, shall be to secure the highest and most harmonious development of his powers to a complete and consistent whole.
— *Humboldt*

PREFACE, *CONTINUED*

Have you ever needed an apt saying to carry you through a difficult day or to help you solve a problem? Within the covers of this book you will find the answers to many of your problems. You will find enlightenment that will arouse your imagination. Great thoughts are valuable not only for the truth which they contain but also for the truth which they suggest. The wise person opens his mind to the genius and spirit of the world's great ideas. He will feel inspired with the purest and noblest thoughts that have ever animated the human spirit . . . for no one is alone who is accompanied by noble thoughts.

He is a benefactor of mankind who contracts the great rules of life into short sentences, that may be easily impressed on the memory, and so recur habitually to the mind. — *Samuel Johnson*

The compiler-editor of this book has been out on the front lines of business for over forty years and has seen the need for instruction and guidance in the business of daily living and the making of better men. The main thought behind the compiling of the distilled wisdom of great men and women was to pick out the practical thoughts that apply to the ART and WISDOM of living the HIGHEST and BEST LIFE. The task was to produce a work that should embrace quality, not quantity. This book is dedicated to making you a better person. It will help you to help yourself.

The most important thing has not been learned: How to conduct ourselves so that we may live. — *John Schindler, M.D.*

There are many ways a work of this character can become priceless to you. Take the best thoughts on the topic selected; read them, underline them, repeat them, and make them your own.

If we did all the things we are capable of doing, we would literally astound ourselves. — *Thomas Alva Edison*

PREFACE, *CONTINUED*

Keep this book available on your desk or on the family table where it is in plain sight and can be picked up and read a little at each opportunity. It is a book to brighten each day!

WORDS OF WISDOM TO LIVE BY is literally a chest of jewels for your office or home. It is for everyone who wants to grow . . . for students, businessmen, writers and speakers . . . for all who reach out for HAPPINESS and SUCCESS! Your life will be richer, fuller, and more enjoyable as you share in the wisdom gathered in these pages.

Alfred Armand Montapert
Los Angeles, California

"I QUOTE OTHERS ONLY IN ORDER THE
BETTER TO EXPRESS MYSELF."
—Michel de Montaigne

ABIDE

HE that dwelleth in the secret place of the most High shall abide under the shadow of the Almighty. — *Psalm 91:1*

IF ye abide in me, and my words abide in you, ye shall ask what ye will, and it shall be done unto you. — *John 15:7*

ABILITY

THERE is only one proof of ability ... results. Men with ability in action get results. — *Harry F. Banks*

EACH man has his own vocation; his talent is his call. There is one direction in which all space is open to him.
— *Ralph Waldo Emerson*

EVERY man was born with the ability to do something well. Every man is a born salesman, accountant, football player, farmer, politician or artist, or something. The individual who uses the ability he was given when he was put on this earth ... who works to the very limit of that ability ... is doing what the Lord intended him to do.
— *George Allen*

THE CREATOR has not given you a longing to do that which you have no ABILITY to do. — *O.S. Marden*

PEOPLE of mediocre ABILITY sometimes achieve outstanding success because they don't know when to quit. Most men succeed because they are determined to. — *Alfred A. Montapert*

SKILL to do comes of doing. — *Ralph Waldo Emerson*

ABILITY

THEY are able because they THINK they are able.   — *Virgil (Aeneid)*

ABILITY is a poor man's wealth.   — *M. Wren*

WHAT you have in your mind, your talents, your native abilities, no one can take from you. When you die you take them with you. USE them diligently while you are here. Why wait until the shadows of death?   — *Alfred A. Montapert*

YOUR ability to think constructive thoughts, to see ways to serve, is your real fortune.   — *Stella T. Mann*

NO ABILITIES, however splendid, can command success without intense labor and persevering dedication.   — *A.T. Steward*

"COME to the edge," he said. They said, "We are afraid." "Come to the edge," he said. They came. He pushed them . . . and they flew.
                                  — *Guillaume Appolinaire*

ACCEPTANCE

ALWAYS fall in with what you're asked to accept. Take what is given, and make it over your way. My aim in life has always been to hold my own with whatever's going. Not against . . . with.   — *Robert Frost*

WE ought to take everything God puts on us evenly, not comparing and wondering which is more important, or higher or best.
                                  — *Meister Eckhart*

WHAT I can't change I must accept.   — *Alfred A. Montapert*

ACCEPTANCE

BE NOT angry that you cannot make others as you wish them to be . . . since you cannot make yourself as you wish to be.
— *Thomas a Kempis*

ACCOMPLISHMENT

YOU can accomplish much if you don't care who gets the credit.
— *Ronald Reagan*

BEING busy does not always mean real work. The object of all work is production or accomplishment and to either of these ends there must be forethought, system, planning, intelligence and honest purpose, as well as perspiration. Seeming to do is not doing.
— *Thomas Alva Edison*

TRUE success depends . . . more on Character than on Intellect.
— *Alfred A. Montapert*

TO DO today's work well and not to be bothered about tomorrow is the secret of accomplishment.   — *William Osler*

TO ACCOMPLISH great things we must first DREAM, then VISU-ALIZE, then PLAN . . . BELIEVE . . . ACT!   — *Alfred A. Montapert*

REMEMBER that life is not measured in hours, but in accomplishments.   — *James A. Pike*

DO something worth doing.   — *Anonymous*

IT isn't how much you know, but what you get done that the world rewards and remembers.   — *Alfred A. Montapert*

IF life were measured by accomplishments, most of us would die in infancy.   — *A.P. Gouthey*

ACCOMPLISHMENT

THE road to fulfillment in material and spiritual security may prove to be strewn with boulders of difficulty and fallen logs of discouragement. No magic wand or mysterious power will suddenly serve us for the conflicts and contests that life is sure to impose. Each day's experience contributes much to our total accomplishment, as we shall discover when we look down from the steps of achievement.

— *Alfred A. Montapert*

ACCOUNTABILITY

EVERYONE is the son of his own works; i.e., he is responsible for his own acts.

— *Spanish Proverb*

ACHIEVEMENT

A TREE is known by its fruit, a man by his deeds.

— *Anonymous*

THOMAS EDISON is said to have failed 32,000 times in perfecting a single point of the instrument which he invented for the reproduction of the human voice . . . the phonograph. For days on end he did not come out of his laboratory. He had his meals brought to him and when he did sleep he slept on a cot in his laboratory. That is the price of achievement.

I have yet to read the life story of a truly great man, whether he be an artist, a poet, an inventor, a scientist, or a what have you, who did not achieve success by long study and careful planning. Most of them by years of hard work. That is the price of achievement.

— *Alfred A. Montapert*

THERE is no man living who cannot do more than he thinks he can.

— *Henry Ford*

ONLY one who devotes himself to a cause with his whole strength and soul can be a true master. For this reason mastery demands all of a person.

— *Albert Einstein*

ACHIEVEMENT

THE MOST exciting man or woman is the one with a passion or dream. Someone who goes against overwhelming odds to achieve. To such a person, failure is more ennobling than victory. It is a way of proving that person existed. — *James Jones*

ACHIEVEMENTS are the accomplishment of persistent individuals.
— *Alfred A. Montapert*

TRUST yourself. Create the kind of self that you will be happy to live with all your life. Make the most of yourself by fanning the tiny, inner sparks of possibility into the flames of achievement.
— *Foster C. McClellan*

THE WAY to get things done is to have a good assistant.
— *William Feather*

IT is not the critic who counts; not the man who points out how the strong man stumbled, or where the doer of deeds could have done them better. The credit belongs to the man who is actually in the arena, whose face is marred by dust and sweat and blood; who strives valiantly; who errs and comes short again and again; who knows the great enthusiasms, the great devotions; who spends himself in a worthy cause; who at the best, knows in the end the triumph of high achievement, and who, at the worst, if he fails, at least fails while daring greatly, so that his place shall never be with those timid souls who know neither victory nor defeat. — *Theodore Roosevelt*

THE ACHIEVER is the only individual who is truly alive.
— *George Allen*

ACTION

IRON rusts from disuse, stagnant water loses its purity and in cold weather becomes frozen; even so does inaction sap the vigors of the mind. — *Leonardo da Vinci*

ACTION

ACT . . . life is action.
— Oliver Wendell Holmes

IDEAS won't keep: something must be done about them.
— Alfred H. Whitehead

THINGS don't just happen, we make them happen. *— Anonymous*

ACTION does not always bring happiness, but there is no happiness without it. *— Benjamin Disraeli*

THINK your job through, but don't forget that some work must be mixed with the thinking. Thoughts without action are sterile.
— Alfred A. Montapert

THE WISE see knowledge and action as one; they see truly.
— Bhagavad-Gita

THINKING is easy, acting is difficult, and to put one's thoughts into action is the most difficult thing in the world. *— Goethe*

GOD has endowed us all with the potential equipment for rich, full, and successful living. But we must not only realize this truth; we must act on it, we must put God's powers into action in our life.
— Cleda Reyner

"WELL DONE" is better than "well said." *— Anonymous*

ACTION is the final and only true test of a man's capacity.
— Alfred A. Montapert

ADVENTURES

IT is always the adventurers who accomplish great things.
— Montesquieu

PEOPLE must learn to gather adventures and experiences rather than things or possessions. Possessions will burden you; adventures become memories which will enrich your soul and last forever.
— *Alfred A. Montapert*

THE ROAD of life can only reveal itself as it is traveled, each turn in the road brings surprise. Man's future is hidden. — *Anonymous*

ADVERSITY

IT is the north wind that made the Vikings. — *Scandinavian Proverb*

THE GREATER the difficulty, the more glory in surmounting it. Skillful pilots gain their reputation from storms and tempests.
— *Epicurus*

MANY men of great promise fail to achieve strong character for want of a great trial. When adversity does come . . . as it is sure to . . . they fall all to pieces for want of fiber that only testing and drudgery can build into them. The diamond cannot be polished without friction, nor the man perfected without trials. Adversity leads the wise to God and prosperity. — *Alfred A. Montapert*

WHEN it is dark enough, men see the stars. — *Ralph Waldo Emerson*

AGE

WINTER is on my head, but eternal spring is in my heart.
— *Victor Hugo*

OLD AGE is fifteen years older than I am. — *Oliver Wendell Holmes*

AGE

A PERSON'S chronological age is not nearly as important as how he sees himself. You can be full in years but young in spirit. How you see yourself is often related to what you do with yourself. And what you do with yourself is often related to how you feel. As a person becomes older he has less energy for purely physical reasons. However, your mind can remain sharp and clear if you have not had any illnesses or diseases. Age has its compensation; you can increase your quality of enjoyment for you are rich in experience. The most important thing is not just to add years to life, but to add life to your years.
— *Alfred A. Montapert*

THE evening of a well-spent life brings its lamps with it.
— *Joseph Joubert*

I SHALL grow old, but never lose life's zest, Because the road's last turn will be the best.
— *Henry Van Dyke*

THERE are three things that grow precious with age: old wood to burn, old books to read, and old friends to enjoy.
— *Old Adage*

IF SOME divinity would confer on me a new grant of life, I would reject the offer without the least hesitation. I have well nigh finished the race, and have no disposition to return to the starting point. I do not mean to imitate those philosophers who represent the condition of human nature as a subject of just lamentation. The satisfactions of this life are many; but there comes a time when we have had a sufficient measure of its enjoyments, and may well depart contented with our share of the feast. I am far from regretting that this life was bestowed on me; and I have the satisfaction of knowing that I have employed it in such a manner as not to have lived in vain. In short, I consider this world as a place which Nature never intended for my permanent abode; and I look on my departure from it, not as being driven from my habitation, but simply as leaving an inn.
— *Cicero*

AGE

AGE is bound to bring some wrinkles, but none of them should be from worry. *— Alfred A. Montapert*

WRINKLES should merely indicate where smiles have been.
— Mark Twain

DO YOU count your birthdays thankfully? Forgive your friends? Grow gentler and better with advancing years? *— Horace*

AIM

IT is not enough to aim . . . you must hit. *— Italian Proverb*

HIGH aims form high characters, and great objectives bring out great minds. *— Tryon Edwards*

MAN'S aim in life is not to add from day to day to his material prospects and to his material possessions, but his predominant calling is from day to day to come nearer his Maker. *— Mahatma Gandhi*

QUESTION: How can I achieve the most and best with my life? Find a purpose . . . an aim . . . a goal for your life. CHOOSE WHAT YOU MOST OF ALL WANT TO ACCOMPLISH. Evaluate your abilities and field of greatest interest. Set your aim on an underlying purpose that will call forth your finest aspirations and energies.
— Alfred A. Montapert

THE ULTIMATE goal is victory, and if you refuse to work as hard as you possibly can toward that aim, or if you do anything that keeps you from achieving that goal, then you are just cheating yourself.
— Don Shula

AIM

ALWAYS dream and shoot higher than you know you can do. Don't bother just to be better than your contemporaries or predecessors. Try to be better than yourself.
— *William Faulkner*

THERE are two things to aim at in life: first, to get what you want; and, after that, to enjoy it. Only the wisest of mankind achieve the second.
— *Logan Pearsall Smith*

EVEN though we all live under the same sky we do not all have the same horizon. Set your sights and standards HIGH . . . VERY HIGH . . . WINNERS DO!
— *Alfred A. Montapert*

ALTAR

EVERY life needs its altar. It may be in a church or quiet nook, it may be a moment in the day, or a mood of the heart . . . but somewhere the spiritual life must have its altar. From there, life gains its poise and direction.
— *Esther B. York*

AMBITION

THE WORLD steps aside to let any man pass if he knows where he is going.
— *David S. Jordan*

MEN of the greatest abilities are most fired with ambition and, on the contrary, mean and narrow minds are the least actuated by it.
— *Joseph Addison*

PROGRESS is not created by contented people.
— *Frank Tyger*

THINK BIG, do BIG, be BIG.
— *Anonymous*

MODERATE ambition; if we are constantly seeking that which is not reasonably attainable we can NEVER KNOW happiness or contentment. The wise man observes the disastrous results of UNCONTROLLED AMBITIONS, and chooses moderation. It is not necessary to be famous in order to be happy, nor must one be the leading citizen in the community in order to gratify one's social instinct. The ambitious usually pay too much for what they get, and are the most miserable after they get it. — *Alfred A. Montapert*

AMERICA

AMERICA is great because America is good; and if America ever ceases to be good, America will cease to be great.
— *Alexis de Tocqueville*

THE AMERICAN Constitution is the most wonderful work ever performed at a given time by the brain and purpose of man.
— *William E. Gladstone*

OUR country grew up under the tutorship of Christian men and women, who carried the Bible in one hand and conforming conduct in the other. The result was blessings from on high, and the most rapid advancement that any country or civilization ever experienced. Not because of greater resources, but because of conforming to God's eternal varieties of conduct, and when that conduct ceases so also will the blessings. — *Kenneth S. Kleinknecht*

THE AMERICAN republic will endure only so long "as the ideas of the men who founded it continue dominant." — *James Russell Lowell*

WE must face the fact that the United States is neither omnipotent nor omniscient, that we are only six percent of the world's population, and that we cannot right every wrong or reverse each adversity, and that therefore there cannot be an American solution to every world problem. — *John F. Kennedy*

AMERICAN

OUR great strength rests in those high-minded and patriotic Americans whose faith in God and love of country transcend all selfish and self-serving instincts. We must commend their maximum effort toward a restoration to public and private relationships of our age-old standards of morality and ethics . . . a return to the religious fervor which animated our leadership of former years to chart a course of humility and integrity as best to serve the public interest.

— Douglas MacArthur

I WAS born an American; I live an American; I shall die an American; and I intend to perform the duties incumbent upon me in that character to the end of my career.   *— Daniel Webster*

ANALYSIS

GET into the habit of ANALYZING . . . reduce the whole into its parts. Then in time SYNTHESIS will become your habit of mind. You will combine all the parts to form the whole.

— Alfred A. Montapert

ANGER

ANYBODY can become angry . . . that is easy; but to be angry with the right person, and to the right degree, and at the right time, and for the right purpose, and in the right way . . . that is not within everybody's power and is not easy.   *— Aristotle*

WHEN anger rises . . . think of the consequences.   *— Confucius*

ANGER is momentary madness, so control your passion or it will control you.   *— Horace*

ANGER blows out the lamp of the mind. In the examination of a great and important question, everyone should be serene, slow-pulsed and calm.   — *Robert Ingersoll*

THE great remedy for anger is delay.   — *Anonymous*

HOW MANY a day has been dampened and darkened by an angry word.   — *John Lubbock*

I HAVE learned through bitter experience the one supreme lesson: to conserve my anger, and as heat conserved is transmuted into energy, even so our anger controlled can be transmuted into a power which can move the world.   — *Mahatma Gandhi*

ANGER is never without a reason but seldom with a good one.
                                            — *Benjamin Franklin*

FEW men can afford to be angry.   — *Edmund Burke*

EVERY time you get angry, you poison your own system.
                                            — *Alfred A. Montapert*

NO man can think clearly when his fists are clenched.
                                            — *George Jean Nathan*

ANIMALS

ANIMALS are reliable, many full of love, true in their affections, predictable in their actions, grateful and loyal. Difficult standards for people to live up to. I love animals.   — *Alfred A. Montapert*

THE ANIMALS of the earth are among God's special creatures; they help us to work, carry us, guard our homes, and best of all, they bring us Joy and Laughter.   — *St. Francis of Assisi*

ANTICIPATION

NOTHING is as good as it seems beforehand.   — *George Eliot*

DON'T take off your shoes until you get to the creek.   — *Anonymous*

ANXIETY

IT has been said that our anxiety does not empty tomorrow of its sorrows, but only empties today of its strength. — *Charles H. Spurgeon*

ANYWAY

PEOPLE are unreasonable, illogical and self-centered. Love them anyway. If you do good, people will accuse you of selfish, ulterior motives. Do good anyway. If you are successful, you will win false friends and true enemies. Succeed anyway. The good you do today will be forgotten tomorrow. Do good anyway. Honesty and frankness make you vulnerable. Be honest and frank anyway. The biggest men with the biggest ideas can be shot down by the smallest men with the smallest minds. Think big anyway. People favor underdogs but follow only top dogs. Fight for some underdogs anyway. What you spend years building may be destroyed overnight. Build anyway. People really need help but may attack you if you help them. Help them anyway. Give the world the best that you have and you'll get kicked in the teeth. Give the world the best you have anyway.

    — *Anonymous*

APPLICATION

TO LIVE is not only to learn, but to apply. Everything is a matter of proper application.   — *Alfred A. Montapert*

APPRECIATION

THE GREATEST of all gifts is the power to estimate things at their true worth. — *La Rochefoucauld*

GIVE me the ability to see good things in unexpected places and talents in unexpected people. And give me, O Lord, the Grace to tell them so. — *17th Century Nun*

ARGUMENT

WHEN two quarrel, both are to blame. — *Dutch Proverb*

ARGUMENT is the worst sort of conversation. — *Jonathan Swift*

THE thing to do is supply light and not heat. — *Woodrow Wilson*

I NEVER make the mistake of arguing with people for whose opinions I have no respect. — *Edward Gibbon*

ARROGANCE

ARROGANCE is the obstruction of wisdom. — *Bion*

ART

A PAINTER told me that nobody could draw a tree without in some sort becoming a tree; or draw a child by studying the outlines of its form merely . . . but by watching for a time his motions and plays, the painter enters into his nature and can then draw him at will in every attitude. — *Ralph Waldo Emerson*

ART

THE PURSUIT of the artist is unselfish, the beauty he creates is his reward.
— *Felix Adler*

TRUE ART is characterized by an irresistible urge in the creative artist.
— *Albert Einstein*

ART arises when the secret vision of the artist and the manifestation of nature agree to find new shapes.
— *Kahlil Gibran*

ART is the path of the creator to his work.
— *Ralph Waldo Emerson*

ASK

ASK, and it shall be given you; Seek, and ye shall find; Knock, and it shall be opened unto you. For every one that asketh receiveth; And he that seeketh findeth; And to him that knocketh it shall be opened.
— *Luke 11:9-10*

HITHERTO have ye asked nothing in my name: ask, and ye shall receive, that your joy may be full.
— *John 16:24*

KNOW how to ask. There is nothing more difficult for some people. Nor for others, easier.
— *Baltasar Gracian*

ASPIRATIONS

AH, but a man's reach should exceed his grasp, or what's a heaven for?
— *Robert Browning*

I ALWAYS entertain great hopes.
— *Robert Frost*

LORD, grant me that I may always desire more than I can accomplish.
— *Michelanglo*

LET this be your slogan: "Make your plans BIG."
— *Alfred A. Montapert*

BEWARE what you set your heart upon. For it shall surely be yours.
— *Ralph Waldo Emerson*

TO UNDERSTAND the heart and mind of a person, look not at what he has already achieved, but at what he aspires to do. — *Kahlil Gibran*

If a man is to get anywhere in life, his aspirations must be fairly constant. Having marked out a course for himself in life, a man must hold to it. A temporary setback or disappointment must not be allowed to turn us from our purpose. Many of the bitter failures stalking around in this world have done enough drudgery in a dozen different occupations to have won them great success if their efforts had all been concentrated on a single line of endeavor.
— *Alfred A. Montapert*

ASSOCIATE

ASSOCIATE with men of good quality, if you esteem your own reputation; it is better to be alone than in bad company.
— *George Washington*

NO MAN is great in and of himself. You must touch great men who can lift you, push you forward and give you confidence.
— *Distilled Wisdom*

KEEP away from people who try to belittle your ambition. Small people always do that, but the really great make you feel that you, too, can become great.
— *Mark Twain*

ASSOCIATE

BE civil to all; sociable to many; familiar with few.

— Benjamin Franklin

FINALLY, my brethren, be strong in the Lord, and in the power of his might. Put on the whole armour of God, that ye may be able to stand against the wiles of the devil.   *— Ephesians 6:10-11*

THOSE who sleep with dogs will rise with fleas.   *— Italian Proverb*

ATHEIST

AN ATHEIST is a man who has no invisible means of support.

— John Buchan

THERE are no atheists in foxholes.   *— William T. Cummings*

THE fool hath said in his heart, There is no God.   *— Psalm 14:1*

MAN WORSHIPS OVER 3000 GODS. No man is an atheist. He worships some god or gods. If he does not subscribe to the Biblical statement of the Eternal God, he will create a god to which he will render his undivided allegiance. He may not "go to church" but he will, nevertheless, attend a church of his own making. He may call himself an atheist but he is, in reality, a devout believer. He may flatter himself that he does not "believe in prayer" but he is, finally, a devout man of faith. He must worship SOMETHING: He's built that way. If not the God revealed in the Bible, then the gods of the State, Success, Money, Power, Fame, Education, Sex, Work, Laziness, Pleasure, Possessions, Gambling, Narcotics, Idols, Drunkenness, Gluttony, Pride. Of course, he does not call them "God" but they command the same devotion that a believer renders to the True God . . . and, alas, sometimes even more and better devotion. But the final hour of life will bring disillusionment. He will find that his god is too small and altogether inadequate.   *— Alfred A. Montapert*

DESPAIR is the only genuine atheism.

— *Jean Paul Richter*

ATTITUDE

MORE players lick themselves by their negative mental attitude than are ever licked by an opposing team. The first thing any man has to know is how to handle himself... by THINKING and ACTING like a WINNER!

— *Connie Mack*

WE should keep our minds friendly to high ideals and noble aspirations. SEE only the good and the beautiful in everything and everybody. Overlook the bad and it will disappear.

— *Alfred A. Montapert*

ADOPTING the right attitude can convert a negative stress into a positive one.

— *Hans Selye*

THAT which you think today becomes that which you are tomorrow.

— *Napoleon Hill*

TO CULTIVATE a joyous and positive atmosphere not only means greater helpfulness to others but also helps us overcome our moods and enables us to move creatively and intelligently beyond them.

— *Hal Lingerman*

WHEN you are thwarted, it is your own attitude that is out of order.

— *Meister Eckhart*

QUESTION: Why are we Masters of our Fate, the captains of our souls? ANSWER: Because we have the POWER to control our THOUGHTS, our ATTITUDES. That is why many people live in the withering negative world. That is why many people live in the Positive Faith World. And you don't have to be a poet or a philosopher to know which is best!

— *Alfred A. Montapert*

ATTITUDE

THE OPTIMIST sees the rose and not its thorns; the pessimist stares at the thorns, oblivious of the rose.   — *Kahlil Gibran*

IT IS only with the heart that one can see rightly; what is essential is invisible to the eye.   — *De Saint Exupery*

THE thinking world is beginning to realize that all the dangers that besiege you can be met with the greatest weapon you possess: your thoughts and your emotions.   — *Walter M. Germain*

MAN is not disturbed by things, but by his opinion about things.
    — *Epictetus*

WE cannot choose the things that will happen to us. But we can choose the attitude we will take toward anything that happens. Success or failure depend on your attitude.   — *Alfred A. Montapert*

A PERSON may, through his own reasoning, develop an attitude towards life that will give a meaning to his existence, a basis of living, and a confidence in his inborn powers to make a better and happier life for himself and others.   — *William Ross*

TAKE away thy opinion, and then there is taken away the complaint, "I have been harmed." Take away the complaint, "I have been harmed," and the harm is taken away.   — *Marcus Aurelius*

HAPPINESS depends not on things around me, but on my ATTITUDE. Everything in my life will depend on my ATTITUDE.
    — *Alfred A. Montapert*

TO one man, the world is barren, dull and superficial, to another rich, interesting and full of meaning.   — *Schopenhauer*

ATTITUDE

The greatest discovery of my generation is that human beings can alter their lives by altering their attitudes of mind.

— William James

ATTITUDES are more important than aptitudes. Attitudes affect your body; we create the climate in and around us by our attitudes. Have a beautiful, warm and friendly attitude. Everything in your life will depend on your attitude. *— Alfred A. Montapert*

ONE thing is sure. You can't have darkness and light in the same place at the same time. The cure for a gloomy outlook is a lighted mind. *— A.P. Gouthey*

THERE is very little difference in people, but that little difference makes a big difference. The little difference is attitude. The big difference is whether it is positive or negative.

— Clement Stone

IF you wish to travel far and fast, travel light. Take off all your envies, jealousies, unforgiveness, selfishness and fears.

— Glenn Clark

HAVE a happy, loving attitude. A mature, positive attitude promotes health. This is the best state of psychological and spiritual health obtainable on this earth. *— Evelyn W. Montapert*

TAKE care that the face which looks out from your mirror in the morning is a pleasant face. You may not see it again during the day, but others will. *— Anonymous*

THE world is so full of care and sorrow that it is a gracious debt we owe to one another to discover the bright crystals of delight hidden in somber circumstances and irksome tasks. *— Helen Keller*

ATTITUDE

OUR project may be 95% perfect, but we focus on the 5% that is bad, negative. We keep our eyes on the obstacles instead of on the main goal. Negative attitudes bring negative results.

— Alfred A. Montapert

THERE'S always some person who thinks the bottom is dropping out of everything . . . and he's usually sitting on his.   *— Dan Valentine*

WHEN you are told you are good, you should not relax but should try to become even better. Your continuous improvement gives happiness to you, to those around you, and to God.

— Paramahansa Yogananda

A MAN'S task is always light if his heart is light.   *— Lew Wallace*

THE winners in life think constantly in terms of I can, I will and I am. Losers, on the other hand, concentrate their waking thoughts on what they should have or would have done, or what they can't do.

— Dr. Dennis Waitley

IF you are doing nothing worth doing, then life is not worth much to you. There is infinitely more joy in honest endeavor than in any surfeit of ease. The bumps and knocks and the hammer blows broaden us. The disappointments and failures enrich our characters. Even our disillusionments should not stop us from trying to "see good in everything."   *— B.C. Forbes*

ATTRACTION

THE MORE one thing is like another, the more it pursues it.

— Meister Eckhart

A MAN is a selecting principle, gathering his like to him wherever he goes.   *— Ralph Waldo Emerson*

ATTRIBUTES

NOTHING in the world can take the place of persistence and determination.
— Calvin Coolidge

MATERIALISTICALLY, the valuable person is the one who has money or tools to use or to lend, or potatoes or skills to sell. Intellectually, the valuable person is the one who has knowledge and understanding which are available to others in search of knowledge and understanding. Spiritually, the valuable person is the one who, by reason of a love of righteousness, discovers some of the divine principles of the universe and becomes able to impart to others that which he has perceived . . . by deed as well as by word.
— Leonard E. Read

A "MUSICAL VOICE," a "magnetic personality," a "winning smile" and a "gift of wit" are without doubt valuable attributes, but none of them, nor all of them, make a dependable leader.
— Alfred A. Montapert

HE who has health has hope; and he who has hope, has everything.
— Arabian Proverb

ELEGANCE is necessary to the fine gentleman, dignity is proper to noble men, and majesty to kings.
— William Hazlitt

AVOID

LET a man avoid evil deeds as a man who loves life avoids poison.
— Buddha

SHUN worthless associates with their empty talk and mundane ambitions.
— Buddha

AVOID

DO not consider anything for your interest which makes you break your word, quit your modesty, or inclines you to any practice which will not bear the light or look the world in the face.

— Marcus Aurelius

IF you won't create trouble for yourself, more than half your troubles will be over. *— Anonymous*

AVOID the evil, and it will avoid thee. *— Gaelic Proverb*

EVERYTHING has its beauty, but not everyone sees it. *— Confucius*

AWAKENING

FEW students who seek the knowledge for a complete awakening are willing to prepare themselves to receive it. Only when the mind and body have become purified through Right Thinking, Right Aspirations, and Right Action over a period of time can this awakening be received with safety. *— Laura Ellis*

IF any man be in CHRIST, he is a new creature. *— II Corinthians 5:17*

AWARENESS

THE three ABC's: A = AWARENESS, B = BEFORE, C = CHOICE. *— Alfred A. Montapert*

AS you walk down the fairway of life, you must smell the roses, for you only get to play one round. *— Ben Hogan*

THE greatest of all faults is to be conscious of none. *— Thomas Carlyle*

BAIT

IT matters not how many fish are in the sea . . . if you don't have any bait on your hook.   — *Dail West*

BALANCE

THERE is health when the body is harmonized into unity, and beauty when the essence of unity controls the parts, and virtue in the soul when it is unified and brought into a single harmonious whole.
                                                    — *Plotinus*

WHO finds union of mind and heart will reach immortality.
                                                    — *Lao Tzu*

FIND the right balance in life. Man is body . . . mind . . . spirit. Give the right amount of attention to each.   — *Alfred A. Montapart*

MAN is a living organism, and the health of such an organism demands a proper amount of equilibrium and balance of all its operating parts . . . If our psychological activities are marked chiefly by uncertainty, struggle, and search, our mind and feelings are not performing smoothly; they are, on the contrary, deficient in balance.
                                                    — *Alexis Carrel*

BASHFULNESS

BASHFULNESS is an ornament to youth, but a reproach to old age.
                                                    — *Aristotle*

BATTLES

I ALWAYS knew how great the Victory was going to be . . . by how great the battle was.   — *Oral Roberts*

BATTLES

WE are not supposed to fight our BATTLES by the strength of our will . . . or by what fortitude we can muster . . . BUT by the FAITH of GOD . . . LODGED IN THE HEART OF US.   *— Alfred A. Montapert*

BE

DON'T be an agnostic. Be something.   *— Robert Frost*

IF you try to be somebody by being like everybody . . . you'll be a nobody!   *— Anonymous*

BEAUTY

BEAUTY is as summer fruits, which are easy to corrupt and cannot last.   *— Francis Bacon*

BEAUTY and folly often go together   *— French Proverb*

BEAUTY is worse than wine; it intoxicates both holder and beholder.   *— Johann Von Zimmerman*

NO REASON can be asked or given why the soul seeks beauty. Beauty, in its largest and profoundest sense, is one expression for the universe.   *— Ralph Waldo Emerson*

BEAUTY is life when life unveils her holy face. But you are life and you are the veil. Beauty is eternity gazing at itself in a mirror. But you are eternity and you are the mirror.   *— Kahlil Gibran*

BEAUTY is but the sensible image of the Infinite. Like truth and justice it lives within us; like virtue and the moral law it is a companion of the soul.   *— George Bancroft*

BEAUTY in things exists in the mind which contemplates them.
— *David Hume*

THE LONGER I live the more beautiful life becomes. The earth's beauty grows on men. If you foolishly ignore beauty, you'll soon find yourself without it. Your life will be impoverished. But if you wisely invest in beauty, it will remain with you all the days of your life.
— *Frank Lloyd Wright*

THOUGH we travel the world over to find the beautiful, we must carry it with us or we will find it not. — *Ralph Waldo Emerson*

NEVER lose an opportunity of seeing anything that is beautiful; for beauty is God's handwriting . . . a wayside sacrament. Welcome it in every fair face, in every fair sky, in every fair flower, and thank God for it as a cup of blessing. — *Ralph Waldo Emerson*

BEGINNING

THE first step is the hardest. — *Marie de Vichy-Chamrond*

BEGIN, and you are halfway there. — *Alfred A. Montapert*

A JOURNEY of a thousand miles begins with a single step.
— *Chinese Saying*

BEHAVIOR

BEHAVIOR is a mirror in which everyone shows his own image.
— *Unknown*

THE DOG wags his tail, not for you, but for your bread.
— *Portuguese Proverb*

BELIEF/BELIEVE

BE NOT afraid of life. Believe that life is worth living, and your belief will help create the fact.
— *William James*

ALL I have seen teaches me to trust the Creator for all I have not seen.
— *Ralph Waldo Emerson*

IF you don't have solid beliefs you cannot build a stable life. Beliefs are like the foundation of a building, and they are the foundation to build your life upon.
— *Alfred A. Montapert*

FOR it is the soul that sees, it is the soul and understanding that hears, all the rest are deaf and blind; and like as if there were no sun at all we should live in perpetual darkness.
— *Plutarch of Chaeronia*

MAN is what he believes, for belief is the great force of the mind. To accomplish great things we must DREAM... PLAN... ACT... BELIEVE.
— *Alfred A. Montapert*

THE MEN of the past had convictions, while we moderns have only opinions.
— *H. Heine*

FOR they conquer who believe they can.
— *Virgil*

EXPECT a miracle! Jesus said, "Therefore I say unto you, What things soever ye desire, when ye pray, believe that ye receive them, and ye shall have them."
— *Mark 11:24*

YOU must BELIEVE before you receive... that is FAITH. THE ONLY LIMIT TO THE POWER OF GOD LIES WITHIN YOU.
— *Alfred A. Montapert*

BENEFIT

HE who lives only to benefit himself confers on the world a benefit when he dies.   — *Tertullian*

BEST

THE BEST things in life are not free but priceless.
                                          — *Benjamin Lichtenberg*

THINK only of the best. Work only for the best. Expect only the best.   — *Anonymous*

WHEN we do the best we can, we never know what miracle is wrought in our life, or in the life of another.   — *Helen Keller*

IF you would get life's best . . . see to it that life gets your best.
                                          — *Anonymous*

BEWARE

BEWARE of any theory of government, religious creed, or doctrine or philosophy of life, that incapacitates you for independent thinking and action.   — *A.P. Gouthey*

BEWARE the fury of a patient man.   — *Publilius Syrus*

BIBLE

A BIBLE that is falling apart usually belongs to someone who isn't.
                                          — *Anonymous*

BELIEF in the Bible, the fruit of deep meditation, has served me as the guide of my moral and literary life. I have found it a capital safely invested, and richly productive of interest.   — *Goethe*

BIBLE

THERE IS ONLY ONE BOOK. The truth taught by the BIBLE is the right way to live. Apart from the LIFE and TEACHINGS of JESUS, Life becomes an unexplained mystery. No marvel then that people who reject Jesus Christ find life "not worth living."

— *Alfred A. Montapert*

ONLY in the GOSPEL is the WHOLE TRUTH. This is the only printed WORD you can really completely believe in.

— *Frederick K. C. Price*

THE BIBLE is a great treasury of reserved blessing. There has not been a chapter, a line, a word, added to it since the pen of inspiration wrote the final Amen; yet every new generation finds new things in this Holy Book. How true it is in every individual experience. As younger people, we study the Bible but many of the precious verses have little or no meaning for us. The light, the comfort, the help are all there, but we do not see it. We cannot see it until we have a fuller sense of need. The rich truths seem to be hiding away, refusing to disclose their meaning. When we begin to experience the struggles, trials, and conflicts of real life, then the new senses begin to reveal themselves in the old familiar sentences. Promises that seemed as if they were written in invisible ink now begin to glow with rich meaning, flash out like newly lighted lamps, and pour bright beams upon the path of life.

— *Mrs. Charles E. Cowman*

ONE of Fouque's most famous fables is the fable of the Magic Mirror. Whoever looked into this mirror could read his character, history and destiny. The Bible is the true magic mirror. It is the Book of insight, foresight, and farsight. It reveals the depth of our degradation, our possible elevation through redemption, and the timelessness of our fellowship with Him who said, "I am." When God would do the greatest possible thing for men, He, in the person of Jesus Christ, made this Book a living thing among us and showed us how to live the life we were created to live.

— *The Supreme Philosophy Of Man*

THE BIBLE is the best guide to life. — *Anonymous*

THE longer you read the Bible, the more you will like it; it will grow sweeter and sweeter; and the more you get into the spirit of it, the more you will get into the spirit of Christ. — *William Romaine*

BLESSINGS

BLESSINGS are not valued until they are gone. — *Thomas Fuller*

REFLECT upon your present blessings, of which every man has many . . . not on your past misfortunes, of which all men have some.
— *Charles Dickens*

WE are most of us very lonely in this world; you who have any who love you, cling to them and thank God. — *William M. Thackeray*

IF YOU want to feel rich, just count all of the things you have that money can't buy. — *Anonymous*

BODY

EVERY man is the builder of a temple, called his body.
— *Henry David Thoreau*

BOLD

WHATEVER you can do, or dream you can, begin it. Boldness has genius, power and magic in it. — *Goethe*

THE wicked flee when no man pursueth; but the righteous are bold as a lion. — *Proverbs 28:1*

FORTUNE favors the bold. — *Virgil*

BOOKS

A MAN is himself . . . plus the books he reads.

— Alfred A. Montapert

BOOKS, like friends, should be few and well chosen.   *— Joineriana*

A MAN'S best library: A Bible and a dictionary.   *— Unknown*

MANY useful and valuable books lie buried in shops and libraries unknown and unexamined, unless some lucky compiler opens them by chance, and finds an easy spoil of wit and wisdom.

— Samuel Johnson

THE BEST service a book can render you is, not to impart truth, but to make you think it out for yourself.   *— Elbert G. Hubbard*

EXCEPT a living man, there is nothing more wonderful than a book.

— Charles Kingsley

IN Books you can read the minds of the best men.

— Alfred A. Montapert

I'M a book person. I'm nurtured in books.   *— Robert Frost*

THE WORLD of books is the most remarkable creation of man. Nothing else that he builds ever lasts. Monuments fall . . . nations perish . . . civilizations grow old and die out. After an era of darkness, people build new nations. But in the world of books there are volumes that live on, still as young and fresh as the day they were written . . . still telling men's thoughts of generations long past.

— Clarence Day

GIVE me health, and a June day and a book and I will put to shame the pageantry of kings.   *— Ralph Waldo Emerson*

IN BOOKS we have the richest treasures ... the legacies that great minds leave to mankind. Through them we put life into our living.
— *Alfred A. Montapert*

BOOKS must be read as deliberately and reservedly as they were written.
— *Henry David Thoreau*

THE BOOKS that help you most are those which make you think the most. The hardest way of learning is that of easy reading; but a great book that comes from a great thinker is a ship of thought, deep freighted with truth and beauty.
— *Theodore Parker*

ALONE, man is an unlighted candle, but a good book lights the candle, stimulates his mind, and rouses each faculty to its most vigorous life.
— *Alfred A. Montapert*

THERE are two motives for reading a book ... one, that you enjoy it; the other, that you can boast about it.
— *Bertrand Russell*

OF the things which man can do or make here below, by far the most momentous, wonderful and worthy are the things we call books!
— *Thomas Carlyle*

EVERY great book has been written with the author's blood.
— *Alfred A. Montapert*

BOREDOM

THE man who lets himself be bored is even more contemptible than the bore.
— *Samuel Butler*

IF you have no goals you will be bored; you will be unhappy because you are empty.
— *Alfred A. Montapert*

THERE are no uninteresting things; there are only uninterested people.
— *G.K. Chesterton*

BRAIN

THE finest piece of mechanism in all the universe is the brain of man. The wise person develops his brain, and opens his mind to the genius and spirit of the world's great ideas. He will feel inspired with the purest and noblest thoughts that have ever animated the spirit of humanity. — *Alfred A. Montapert*

BRIEF

THE MORE you say, the less people remember. The fewer words, the greater the profit. — *Francois Fenelon*

UNLESS you are brief, your complete plan of thought will never be grasped. Before you reach the conclusion, the reader or listener has forgotten the beginning and the middle. — *Horace*

THERE is too much speaking in the world and almost all of it is too long. The Lord's Prayer, the 23rd Psalm, Lincoln's Gettysburg Address are three great literary treasures that will last forever; no one of them is as long as 300 words. With such striking illustrations of the power of brevity, it is amazing that speakers never learn to be brief.

— *Bruce Barton*

BURDENS

SOMETIMES the load we bear may seem very heavy. At times it may seem to be more than we are able to carry. And there is always someone to agree with us that we are really having a rough time. "This is getting to be too much. Why do I always have to bear so much? Why do I get the dirty end of the stick? I know I try to be better than many other people and they prosper. I try to do what is right and never seem to succeed." At this point we must remember that Almighty God never gives us a greater burden than we can bear. He knows how much we can carry. — *Unknown*

BUREAUCRAT

A BUREAUCRAT is a person who can take raw material and turn it into waste. — *Unknown*

BUSINESS

BOLDNESS in business is the first essential, as well as the second, third and fourth. — *Unknown*

BUSINESS is like riding a bicycle. Either you keep moving or you fall down. — *John D. Wright*

SOME day the ethics of business will be universally recognized, and in that day business will be seen to be the oldest and most useful of all the professions. — *Henry Ford*

DRIVE thy business, let not thy business drive thee. — *Benjamin Franklin*

IT'S a bad bargain where nobody gains. — *English Proverb*

ANY business arrangement that is not profitable to the other fellow will in the end prove unprofitable for you. The bargain that yields mutual satisfaction is the only one that is apt to be repeated. — *B.C. Forbes*

ALL lasting business is built . . . on FRIENDSHIP. — *Alfred A. Montapert*

BUSYBODY

BUSY souls have no time to be busybodies. — *Austin O'Malley*

CALENDAR

THE only calendar I need is just outside my window. With eyes to see and ears to hear, Nature keeps me posted.

— Alfred A. Montapert

CALM

CALMNESS is another word for confidence . . . and confidence is faith in action.

— Unknown

CANNES

THE most fascinating amalgamation of wealth, luxury and general uselessness in the world.

— F. Scott Fitzgerald

CAPABILITY

IF we did all the things we are capable of doing, we would literally astound ourselves.

— Thomas Alva Edison

MEN are often capable of greater things than they perform. They are sent into the world with bills of credit, and seldom draw to their full extent.

— Horace Walpole

CAPACITY

FEW of us know what we are capable of doing . . . we have never pushed ourselves hard enough to find out. Only by voluntarily putting ourselves under the lash of necessity shall we discover our full capacity for doing.

— Anonymous

CAPACITY without education is deplorable, and education without capacity is thrown away. — *Saadi*

HOW MUCH education is needed? It is a waste of time and effort to try to make lawyers, teachers, scientists, doctors, or preachers out of people who prefer and are better fitted to become foresters, mechanics, farmers, sailors or chauffeurs. YOU CAN NOT POUR FIVE GALLONS INTO A PINT CAN. THIS IS A LAW OF CAPACITY. — *Alfred A. Montapert*

CARE

IF you think nobody cares if you're alive, try missing a couple of car payments. — *Earl Wilson*

WE all have sufficient strength to endure the misfortunes of others. — *La Rochefoucauld*

CARELESS

CARELESS words are like thistle seed . . . easy to scatter, but impossible to gather up once they are sown. — *Anonymous*

CARELESSNESS is worse than theft. — *Gaelic Proverb*

CARELESSNESS about your way of life . . . bad habits of all kinds . . . bring on a host of troubles. When you break Nature's rules, YOU PAY, sometimes with your life! — *Alfred A. Montapert*

CASH

READY money works great cures. — *French Proverb*

CAUSE AND EFFECT

MAN transforms himself into the things he loves. When the time arrives for his sun to set, he has become that which, during the course of his life, he has, consciously or unconsciously, chosen to be.

— *Alexis Carrel*

WHATSOEVER a man sows, that shall he also reap.

— *Galatians 6:7*

CAUSE and effect, means and end, seed and fruit, cannot be severed; for the effect already blooms in the cause, the end pre-exists in the means, the fruit in the seed. — *Ralph Waldo Emerson*

THE cause is hidden but the effect is evident enough. — *Ovid*

SHALLOW men believe in luck, strong men in CAUSE AND EFFECT. — *Anonymous*

I DO not have to worry whether anyone is "getting away" with anything. I'm not the world's policeman. I know that everyone will experience the consequences of his own acts. If his acts are right, he'll get good consequences; if they're not, he'll suffer for it.

— *Alfred A. Montapert*

WE deal with effects instead of first causes. That is why we never get anything fixed. — *Alfred A. Montapert*

CAUTION

CAUTION is the parent of safety. — *Anonymous*

DRINK nothing without seeing it, sign nothing without reading it.

— *Portuguese Proverb*

CELEBRATION

LET us celebrate the occasion with wine and sweet words.

— Latin Proverb

DRINK champagne for defeats as well as for victories. It tastes the same, and you need it more. *— Edmund Ward*

CHALLENGE

YOU cannot run away from a weakness; you must sometime fight it out or perish. And if that be so, why not now, and where you stand?

— Robert Louis Stevenson

THE most dangerous thing in the world is to try to leap a chasm in two jumps. *— David Lloyd George*

I BELIEVE in getting into hot water. It keeps you clean.

— G. K. Chesterton

CHANCE

CHANCE fights ever on the side of the prudent. *— Euripides*

CHANCE may be the pseudonym God uses when He doesn't want to sign His name. *— Unknown*

CHANGE

ALL change is not progress . . . just as all movement is not forward.

— Alfred A. Montapert

BLESSED is the man who has discovered that there is nothing permanent in life but change. *— A. P. Gouthey*

CHANGE

ONE must never lose time in vainly regretting the past nor in complaining against the changes which cause us discomfort, for change is the very essence of life. — *Anatole France*

EVERYONE thinks of changing the world, but no one thinks of changing himself. — *Leo Tolstoy*

CHARACTER

CHARACTER is made by many acts; it may be lost by a single one. — *Unknown*

WHAT you do when you don't have to, determines what you will be when you can no longer help it. — *Rudyard Kipling*

FAME is a vapor, popularity an accident, riches take wings, those who cheer today will curse tomorrow, only one thing endures... character. — *Horace Greeley*

NOT education, but character, is man's greatest NEED ... and man's greatest safeguard. When the late J.P. Morgan was asked what he considered the best bank collateral, he replied, "Character!" — *Alfred A. Montapert*

INDUSTRY, thrift, and self-control are not sought because they create wealth, but because they create character. — *Calvin Coolidge*

CHARACTER is what I am. Reputation is what people think of me. — *Alfred A. Montapert*

NATURE has written a letter of credit upon some men's faces that is honored wherever presented. You cannot help trusting such men. Their very presence gives confidence. There is "Promise to pay" in their faces which gives confidence and you prefer it to another man's endorsement. Character is credit. — *William M. Thackeray*

CHARACTER

CHARACTER is a by-product; it is produced in the great manufacture of daily duty. — *Woodrow Wilson*

CHARACTER is the scribe that writes your true biography.
— *Alfred A. Montapert*

CHARACTER is higher than intellect. Thinking is the function, living is the functionary. — *Ralph Waldo Emerson*

YOU don't make your character in a crisis, you exhibit it. — *Unknown*

CHARACTER is that which reveals moral purpose, exposing the class of things a man chooses or avoids. — *Aristotle*

THE history of a man is in his character. — *Goethe*

CHARM

A SINCERE interest in other people, an unselfish heart, a desire to make others comfortable and at ease, is the foundation of charm.
— *Anonymous*

CHEERFUL

THE cheerful live longest in years, and afterwards in our regards. Cheerfulness is the offshoot of Goodness. — *Christian N. Bovee*

A CHEERFUL friend is like a sunny day, which sheds its brightness on all around; and most of us can, as we choose, make of this world either a palace . . . or a prison. — *John Lubbock*

CHEERFULNESS

CHEERFULNESS opens, like spring, all the blossoms of the inward man.
— *Jean Paul Richter*

CHEERFULNESS is the best promoter of health, and is as friendly to the mind as to the body.
— *Joseph Addison*

CHILDREN

TRAIN up a child in the way he should go and when he is old he will not depart from it.
— *Proverbs 22:6*

IF you help the children while they're still children, their children will be able to help themselves.
— *Unicef*

CHOICE

CHOOSE this day whom you will serve.
— *Joshua 24:15*

WE make choices, and our choices determine how we come out. Whatsoever we sow, we reap. The Law is, LIKE produces LIKE. Plant corn and you harvest corn, not tomatoes.
— *Alfred A. Montapert*

THERE'S small choice in rotten apples.
— *William Shakespeare*

TO every man and woman is given the power of choice. YOU have the choice of living a mediocre life or the abundant life. Life is actually made up of our choices. We are the sum total of them. CHOICE . . . NOT CHANCE . . . DETERMINES HUMAN DESTINY.
— *Alfred A. Montapert*

CHOOSE the best and habit will make it yours.   — *Francis Bacon*

LIFE is an adventure, not a burden. If others choose to make the world's ills their business, let them. If others choose to fight the politicians' wars, it's unfortunate but that's their choice. It doesn't have to be yours. You can make a wonderful life for yourself. Use the years ahead of you to develop your full potential and keep your freedom and happiness.   — *Alfred A. Montapert*

EVERY person has FREE CHOICE . . . Free to Obey or Disobey the NATURAL LAWS. YOUR CHOICE determines the consequences. NOBODY EVER DID, OR EVER WILL, ESCAPE THE CONSE-QUENCES OF HIS CHOICES.   — *Alfred A. Montapert*

CHRIST

NO other fame can be compared with that of Jesus. He has a place in the human heart that no one who ever lived has in any measure rivaled. No name is pronounced with a tone of such love and veneration. All other laurels wither before his. His are ever kept fresh with tears of gratitude.   — *William E. Channing*

JESUS CHRIST came to this world to bring LOVE. The LOVE taught by the God-Man was the cement to bind all men together in brotherly love and kindness.   — *Alfred A. Montapert*

WHEN all the securities of the world disappear, Jesus Christ is still with you.   — *Corrie Ten Boom*

CHRIST IS THE ANSWER. But, He is not the answer until you experience His resurrection in your heart, and you as an individual start to re-live His life. Then He becomes the answer. Then He becomes to you, as an individual, the way, the truth, and the life.
     — *Anonymous*

CHRIST

JESUS CHRIST made no claims as a philosopher; yet what philosopher ever devised a scheme for living worthy to be compared with His teaching?
— *Anonymous*

CHRISTIAN/CHRISTIANITY

IT is amazing how much religion we can absorb without ever contacting God. It is our business as Christians to relive Christ, among men. What a man DOES is the real test of what a man IS.
— *Alfred A. Montapert*

THE TRUE Christian needs no security other than his faith and a sense of God.
— *A.P. Gouthey*

WHATEVER makes men good Christians, makes them good citizens.
— *Daniel Webster*

CHRISTIANITY is not a philosophy, it's not a doctrine, it's not a creed, it's not a statement of what we call truth which we have learned to repeat. Christianity is a person. It is Christ. "Christ in you," said the Apostle Paul, "is the hope of glory." It's the hope of all into the eternal years.
— *Unknown*

CHRISTIANITY is not a doctrine. It is not a creed that we commit and live by rule and rote. CHRISTIANITY is a WAY OF LIFE. "FOLLOW ME" is the command.
— *John L. Smart*

CHRISTIANITY has a might of its own, it is raised above all philosophy, and needs no support therefrom.
— *Goethe*

THE SERMON on the Mount is one of the greatest systems of psychotherapy that has ever been given. It tells us when we do right, ourselves, and our dedications are right ... Heaven is with us. To have Heaven with us is more important than having all the world with us, if we do wrong.
— *Alfred A. Montapert*

A CHRISTIAN is one who makes it easier for others to believe in God.   — *Anonymous*

CHRISTMAS

THE finest Christmas gift can't be bought, sold, wrapped or refunded. It is the gift of LOVE ... the feeling of peace and good will towards all. LOVE is priceless.   — *Alfred A. Montapert*

SOME DAY – A REAL CHRISTMAS
Some day there will be a real Christmas.
Some day the peoples of the world will rise to
    pay homage to the principles that will assure peace.
But the real Christmas will never come through the electric
    display of slogans or the myriads of tinseled trees
    exhibited along our thoroughfares.
The real Christmas will come when men have discovered
    within themselves the power that overnight can
    frustrate the commands issued by the despots.
The real Christmas will come when, among nations like our
    own and our allies, there is an impulse to follow the
    courageous will of a liberated conscience.
To achieve this emancipation from the shackles of modern
    ideologies, we must grow a Christmas tree that
    doesn't wither the day after Christmas ... a tree that
    is nourished with our own hearts and spreads its
    branches from man to man as it unites us all in a
    world of eternal love.   — *David Lawrence*

CHURCH

WHAT the church should be telling the workman is that the first demand religion makes on him is that he should be a good workman. If he is a carpenter, he should be a good carpenter. He should attend church by all means, but what use is church if, at the very center of life, a man defrauds his neighbor and insults God by poor craftsmanship?   — *Dwight D. Eisenhower*

CIRCUMSTANCES

MAKE the best of your circumstances. No one has everything, and everyone has something of sorrow intermingled with gladness of life. The trick is to make the laughter outweigh the tears.   — *Anonymous*

CIRCUMSTANCES do not create themselves; they are always molded by our thought patterns.   — *Ernest Holmes*

CITIZEN

THE first requisite of a good citizen in this Republic of ours is that he shall be able and willing to pull his weight.   — *Theodore Roosevelt*

THE prosperity of a country depends not on the abundance of its revenues, nor on the strength of its fortifications, nor on the beauty of its public buildings; but it consists in the number of its cultivated citizens, in its men of education, enlightenment, and character; here are to be found its true interest, its chief strength, its real power.
— *Martin Luther*

WE believe that the reduction of the citizen to an object of propaganda, private and public, is one of the greatest dangers to democracy. A prevalent notion is that the great mass of the people cannot understand and cannot form an independent judgement upon any matter; they cannot be educated, in the sense of developing their intellectual powers, but they can be bamboozled. The reiteration of slogans, the distortion of the news, the great storm of propaganda that beats upon the citizen twenty-four hours a day all his life long mean either that democracy must fall a prey to the loudest and most persistent propagandists or that the people must save themselves by strengthening their minds so that they can appraise the issues for themselves.   — *Robert Hutchins*

OUR American heritage is threatened as much by our own indifference as it is by the most unscrupulous office or by the most powerful foreign threat. The future of this republic is in the hands of the American voter. — *Dwight D. Eisenhower*

EVERY citizen owes to the country a vigilant watch and close scrutiny of its public servants and a fair and reasonable estimate of their fidelity and usefulness. Thus is the people's will impressed upon the whole framework of our civil policy . . . municipal, state, and federal. — *Grover Cleveland*

COLLECT

COLLECT adventures and experiences, not things. Things will burden you. Adventures and experiences give you pleasant memories. — *William D. Montapert*

COMMITMENT

THE quality of every man's life has got to be a full measure of that man's personal commitment to excellence and to victory, regardless of what field he may be in. — *Vince Lombardi*

COMMUNICATION

GOOD writers set forth their thoughts in straightforward sentences. In the same manner, the easiest speakers to understand are those who express themselves in simple, crystal clear sentences, and do not digress from their point. — *The Royal Bank Letter*

YOU can't make anyone FEEL what you don't FEEL. — *Anonymous*

COMPANION

A HARD stretch of road is always made easier by a good traveling companion.
— *Anonymous*

GROW old along with me; the best is yet to be,
The last of life for which the first was made.
— *Robert Browning*

NO possession is gratifying without a companion.
— *Seneca*

THE goodness of companionship consists in human heartedness.
— *Lao-Tze*

COMPANY

TELL me thy company and I will tell thee what thou art.
— *Miguel de Cervantes*

WHAT does one do when one finds oneself unavoidably thrown into bad company? Hold your tongue and use your legs.
— *A. P. Gouthey*

COMPASSION

WHEN you see misery in your brother's face, let him see mercy in yours.
— *Unknown*

THE nobler a soul is, the more objects of compassion it hath.
— *John Morley*

COMPLIMENT

IF you wish to be popular, tell a man how smart you think he is, and a woman how beautiful.
— *Alfred A. Montapert*

I CAN live for two months on a good compliment.   *— Mark Twain*

COMPREHENSION

A MAN hears only what he understands.   *— Goethe*

COMPROMISE

ONE of the most important trips a man can make is that involved in meeting the other fellow halfway.   *— Bruce Von Horn*

BETTER is a lean agreement than a fat lawsuit.   *— German Proverb*

NEVER compromise a PRINCIPLE or relinquish a VITAL TRUTH.
— Alfred A. Montapert

MEN are never so likely to settle a question rightly as when they discuss it freely.   *— Thomas B. Macaulay*

CONCEIT

THE fellow who thinks he knows it all is especially annoying to those of us who do.   *— Harold Coffin*

CONCENTRATION

WHEN every physical and mental resource is focused, one's power to solve a problem multiplies tremendously. To win in this life you simply have to give your all, every bit of yourself ... Life cannot deny itself to the person who gives life everything.
— Norman Vincent Peale

CONCLUSIONS

ALWAYS discern between facts and opinions. You may have all the facts but reach the wrong conclusions. A conclusion is no more correct than the process used in its arrivation, even though the base may be a fact.
— Alfred A. Montapert

CONDUCT

QUIET persons are welcome everywhere.
— Thomas Fuller

WE must learn how to conduct ourselves so that we will know how to live and live well.
— Alfred A. Montapert

A MAN is known by his conduct to his wife, to his family and to those under him.
— Napoleon Bonaparte

CONFESSION

CONFESSED faults are half mended.
— Scotch Saying

CONFIDENCE

I AM not afraid of tomorrow, for I have seen yesterday, and I love today.
— William A. White

DEVELOPING confidence in ourselves, in our ability to meet and handle all undesirable situations, requires that we must have confidence in that Something which is greater than we are.
— Ernest Holmes

I HAVE great faith in those who have great faith in themselves. I know that men who fear themselves are not fit for responsibility.
— Charles M. Schwab

CONSCIENCE

THERE is no pillow so soft as a clear conscience. — *French Proverb*

CONSCIENCE is the voice of the soul; the passions, of the body.
— *Jean Jacques Rousseau*

A SMALL weak voice that is getting smaller and weaker every day. Conscience is the divine part of ourselves, the voice of the heart based upon the evidence of the past and a careful consideration of the Ten Commandments, The Golden Rule and man's total experience of existence. — *Alfred A. Montapert*

LABOUR to keep alive in your breast that little spark of celestial fire . . . conscience. — *George Washington*

CONTENTMENT

THE secret of contentment is knowing how to enjoy what you have, and be able to lose all desire for things beyond your reach.
— *Lin Yutang*

CONTENTMENT is natural wealth. — *Socrates*

DO thine own task, and be therewith content. — *Goethe*

WHEN you get a thing the way you want it . . . leave it alone.
— *Winston Churchill*

IS it not true that my life with all its limitations touches at many points the life of the World Beautiful? Everything has its wonders, even darkness and silence, and I learn, whatever state I may be in, therein to be content. — *Helen Keller*

CONTENTMENT consists not in great wealth, but in few wants.
— *Epictetus*

I HAVE learned, in whatsoever state I am, therewith to be content.
— *Paul Philippians 4:11*

CONTENTMENT

I HAVE learned that to be with those I like is enough.
— *Walt Whitman*

A HEARTH of one's own and a good wife are as good as gold and pearls.
— *German Proverb*

A MAN should always consider how much he has more than he wants and how much more unhappy he might be than he really is.
— *Joseph Addison*

TO BE content, look backward on those who possess less than yourself, not forward on those who possess more. If this does not make you content, you don't deserve to be happy.
— *Benjamin Franklin*

CONTENTMENT does not come to those whose means are great, but to those whose needs are few.
— *Manly Hall*

I WISH so to live ever as to derive my satisfactions and inspirations from the commonest events, everyday phenomena, so that what my senses hourly perceive, my daily walk, the conversation of my neighbors, may inspire me, and I may dream of no heaven but that which lies about me.
— *Henry David Thoreau*

IF a man is moderate and content, then even age is no burden; if he is not, then even youth is full of cares.
— *Plato*

MOST of us are more in need of a deeper sense of contentment with life as it is, than we are of a deeper understanding of life.
— *Alfred A. Montapert*

CONVERSATION

SPEAK but little and well, if you would be esteemed as a man of merit.
— *French Saying*

COST

IT'S not what you pay a man, but what he costs you that counts.
— *Will Rogers*

THE cost of a thing is the amount of my life I spend to obtain it.
— *Alfred A. Montapert*

COURAGE

COWARDS die many times before their death. The valiant never taste of death but once. — *William Shakespeare*

ONE MAN with courage makes a majority. — *Andrew Jackson*

COURAGE consists not in blindly overlooking danger, but in meeting it with the eyes open. — *Jean Paul Richter*

EVERY man is bold when his whole fortune is at stake.
— *Dionysus of Halicarnassus*

COURTESY

COURTESY is that quality of heart that overlooks the broken garden gate and calls attention to the flowers beyond the gate. — *Anonymous*

LIFE is not so short but that there is always time for courtesy.
— *Ralph Waldo Emerson*

COURTESY is the lubricant that eases friction among human beings. Making other people feel good makes us feel good too. Try to act with LOVE for the feelings and well-being of others, then you will know how to be courteous. — *Alfred A. Montapert*

COVETOUS

THE covetous person lives as if the world were made altogether for him and not he for the world, to take in everything and part with nothing.
— *Caleb C. Colton*

THE covetous man keeps up riches, not to enjoy them, but to have them.
— *John Tillotson*

CREATIVITY

THE truly creative mind in any field is no more than this: A human creature born abnormally, inhumanly sensitive. To him a touch is a blow, a sound is a noise, a misfortune is a tragedy, a joy is an ecstasy, a friend is a lover, a lover is a god, and failure is death. Add to this cruelly delicate organism the overpowering necessity to create, create, create . . . so that without the creating of music or poetry or books or building or something of meaning, his very breath is cut off from him. He must create, must pour out creation. By some strange, unknown, inward urgency he is not really alive unless he is creating.
— *Pearl S. Buck*

EVERY act of creation is first of all an act of destruction.
— *Pablo Picasso*

CREATIVITY is a yearning for immortality.
— *Rollo May*

WELCOME, O Life! I go to encounter for the millionth time the reality of experience and to forge in the smithy of my soul the uncreated conscience of my race.
— *James Joyce*

THE more the Soul lives in the light of the Spirit, 'turned towards' that which is above itself, the more creative it becomes.
— *Plotinus*

CREED

HERE is my creed. I believe in one God. Creator of the Universe. That He governs it by His Providence. That He ought to be worshipped. That the most acceptable service we render Him is doing good to His other children. That the soul of man is immortal, and will be treated with justice in another life respecting its conduct in this life.   — *Benjamin Franklin*

AN EVERYDAY CREED: I believe in my job. I believe in my fellow man. I believe in my country. I believe in today.
                                          — *Rev. Charles Stelzle*

CRIME

HE who does not prevent a crime encourages it.   — *Seneca*

CRIMES generally punish themselves.   — *Oliver Goldsmith*

CRIME, like virtue, has its degrees.   — *Racine*

IT is the crime which causes shame, not the scaffold. — *French Saying*

CRISIS

CRISES bring out the best in the best of us . . . and the worst in the worst of us.   — *Anonymous*

CRITICISM

IF you must speak ill of another, do not speak it . . . write it in the sand near the water's edge.   — *Napoleon Hill*

CRITICISM

IT does not require much intelligence or time to raze a building. Quite the contrary is true in its construction. The same is true with criticism versus praise. — *Anonymous*

I HAVE yet to find the man, however exalted his station, who did not do better work and put forth greater effort under a spirit of approval, than under a spirit of criticism. — *Charles Schwab*

IT is much easier to be critical than to be correct. — *Benjamin Disraeli*

THE legitimate aim of criticism is to direct attention to the excellent. — *Christian N. Bovee*

CULTURE

THE value of culture is its effect on character. It avails nothing unless it ennobles and strengthens that. Its use is for life. Its aim is not beauty but goodness. — *Somerset Maugham*

CULTURE is to know the best that has been said and thought in the world. — *Matthew Arnold*

CURIOSITY

CURIOSITY is a necessity of our nature, a blind impulse that obeys no rule . . . Curiosity impels us to discover the universe. — *Alexis Carrel*

CYNIC

A CYNIC is a man who knows the price of everything and the value of nothing. — *Oscar Wilde*

DEATH

DEATH is a doorway not a wall. — *William D. Montapert*

THE reports of my death are greatly exaggerated.
— *Mark Twain*

A USELESS life is an early death. — *Goethe*

YEA, though I walk through the valley of the shadow of death, I will fear no evil; for Thou art with me; Thy rod and Thy staff they comfort me. — *Psalm 23:4*

DEATH'S but a path that must be trod, If man would ever pass to God. — *Thomas Parnell*

DEATH is but another phase of life, which also is awful, fearful, and wonderful, reaching to heaven and hell.
— *Thomas Carlyle*

DEATH comes equally to us all, and makes us all equal when it comes. — *John Donne*

YOU will never understand Life, until you understand Death. Death is a Part of Life, in fact it is the best part of Life ... if you are prepared for it. — *Alfred A. Montapert*

DEATH is the beginning of another life.
— *Michel de Montaigne*

OH, for the touch of a vanished hand, And the sound of a voice that is still! — *Alfred Lord Tennyson*

IT is the beginning of the end. — *Talleyrand*

DEBT

HE is rich enough who owes nothing. — *French Proverb*

THERE are but two ways of paying a debt: increase of industry in raising income, or increase of thrift in laying out.
— *Thomas Carlyle*

DECISIONS

BEFORE a person makes a decision or gets involved he should form the habit of asking himself a simple but important question: "How will this affect my life, and others?" — *Alfred A. Montapert*

THE way to develop decisiveness is to start right where you are, with the very next question you face. — *Napoleon Hill*

TAKE time to deliberate, but when the time for action has arrived, stop thinking and go in. — *Napoleon Bonaparte*

WE make our decision, and then our decisions turn round and make us. — *F. W. Boreham*

DECEPTION

A MAN may smile, and smile, and be a villain.
— *William Shakespeare*

THE senses do not deceive, but the judgment does. — *Goethe*

DECEIVE not thy physician, confessor, nor lawyer.
— *George Herbert*

DEEDS

DEEDS are fruits, words are leaves.

— Anonymous

DEFEAT

HE that strives against Nature will forever strive in vain.

— Samuel Johnson

DEFECT

THE GOOD are befriended even by weakness and defect. As no man had ever a point of pride that was not injurious to him, so no man had ever a defect that was not somewhere made useful to him.

— Ralph Waldo Emerson

DELAY

BY the street of By-and-By, one arrives at the House-of-Never.

— Miguel de Cervantes

DESIRE

THE thirst of desire is never filled, nor fully satisfied. *— Cicero*

THE significance of a man is not in what he attains, but rather what he longs to attain. *— Kahlil Gibran*

WINNING isn't everything, but wanting to win is. *— Arnold Palmer*

LORD, grant that I may always desire more than I accomplish.

— Michelangelo

DESTINY

EXISTENTIALISM is not a pessimistic description of man . . . there is no doctrine more optimistic, since man's destiny is within himself.
— *Jean Paul Sartre*

MAN'S ultimate destiny is to become one with the Divine Power which governs and sustains the creation and its creatures.
— *Alfred A. Montapert*

IF one would know one's destiny, one has only to examine his passions. — *A. P. Gouthey*

IT is a mistake to look too far ahead. Only one link in the chain of destiny can be handled at a time. — *Sir Winston Churchill*

MAN has a destiny to which all his life and activities are directed.
— *St. Thomas Aquinas*

DESTROY

THE THINGS that will destroy us are: politics without principle; pleasure without conscience; wealth without work; knowledge without character; business without morality; science without humanity; and worship without sacrifice. — *Mahatma Gandhi*

IN order to destroy a man, it is only necessary to give his work the character of uselessness. — *Schopenhauer*

WHEN a man wantonly and wastefully destroys one of the works of man we call him a vandal. When he wantonly and wastefully destroys one of the works of God we call him a sportsman.
— *Anonymous*

DEVIL

IT is wonderful how much time good people spend fighting the devil. If they would only expend the same amount of energy loving their fellow men, the devil would die in his own tracks of ennui.

— *Helen Keller*

DIFFERENCE

ONE half of the world laughs at the other half. — *German Saying*

DIFFICULTIES

MANY men owe the grandeur of their lives to their tremendous difficulties. — *Alfred A. Montapert*

DIFFICULTIES are things that show what men are. — *Epictetus*

DIFFICULTIES increase the nearer we approach the goal.

— *Goethe*

DILIGENCE

LET not him who is houseless pull down the house of another, but let him work diligently and build one for himself, thus by example assuring that his own shall be safe from violence when built.

— *Abraham Lincoln*

DILIGENT working makes an expert workman. — *Danish Proverb*

BE like a postage stamp, stick to one thing until you get there.

— *Josh Billings*

DIRECTION

IF you don't know where you are going, you will end up somewhere else.
— Laurence J. Peter

I FIND the great thing in this world is not so much where we stand, as in what direction we are moving. To reach the port of heaven, we must sail sometimes with the wind and sometimes against it ... but we must sail, and not drift, nor lie at anchor. *— Oliver Wendell Holmes*

IF you look back too much, you will soon be heading that way.
— Anonymous

DISCIPLINE

HE that spareth his rod hateth his son: but he that loveth him chasteneth him betimes .
— Proverbs 13:24

I HAVE never known a really successful man who did not understand the grind, the discipline that it takes to win. *— Vince Lombardi*

MAKE it a point to do something every day that you don't want to do. This is the golden rule for acquiring the habit of doing your duty without pain.
— Mark Twain

FOR years we have listened to some quack theorists and pseudopsychologists who have preached that discipline and control were bad for children ... that they should be left uninhibited to work out their own life patterns, their own self-discipline. But you don't acquire self-discipline if you never learn what discipline is. Neither can life's problems be worked out without experience, which can be secured only through hard knocks, or by guidance from the experience of others. Now we are reaping the harvest. *— J. Edgar Hoover*

DISCOURAGEMENT

DISCOURAGEMENT is the common denominator of all unhappy lives.
— *W. Beran Wolfe*

DISCOVERY

WHEN I want to discover something, I begin by reading up everything that has been done along that line in the past . . . that's what all these books in the library are for. I see what has been accomplished at great labor and expense in the past. I gather the data of many thousands of experiments as a starting point, and then I make thousands more.
— *Thomas Alva Edison*

DISCRETION

IT is better to be silent and thought a fool, than to speak and remove all doubt.
— *Silvan Engel*

YOU should not say it is not good. You should say that you do not like it; and then, you know, you're perfectly safe. — *James M. Whistler*

THE heart of the righteous studieth to answer: but the mouth of the wicked poureth out evil things.
— *Proverbs 15:28*

IT IS as important to know when to stop talking as when to start.
— *Alfred A. Montapert*

A LOVER without discretion is no lover at all.
— *Thomas Hardy*

HE who knows not, knows a good deal if he knows how to hold his tongue.
— *Anonymous*

DISTRIBUTION

FREE enterprise is an unequal distribution of blessings and socialism is an equal distribution of misery. — *Winston S. Churchill*

DOING/DOING GOOD

WISDOM is knowing what to do next, Skill is knowing how to do it, and Virtue is doing it. — *Anonymous*

HE who enjoys doing, and enjoys doing what he has done, is happy. — *Goethe*

IN nothing do men more nearly approach the gods than in doing good to their fellow men. — *Cicero*

ALWAYS do right; this will gratify some people and astonish the rest. — *Mark Twain*

DREAMS

IN your wagers with the world, put your bets on dreams, not ideas. — *William D. Montapert*

I PREFER to be a dreamer among the humblest, with visions to be realized, than lord among those without dreams and desires. — *Kahlil Gibran*

WE have all got our "good old days" tucked away inside our hearts, and we return to them in dreams, like cats to favorite armchairs. — *Brian Carter*

WE should be poor indeed if we should dream no dreams, if we should see no visions, if we should be unable to take a long-distance view of life. For in a very real sense our dreams decide our goals in life and our destiny in the life hereafter. — *Alfred A. Montapert*

IT may be those who do most, dream most. — *Stephen Leacock*

NO DREAM comes true until you wake up and go to work.
— *Anonymous*

MAN is no greater than his DREAMS . . . his ideal, his hope, and his plan. Man dreams the dream . . . and fulfilling it, it's the DREAM that makes the man! — *Alfred A. Montapert*

DUTY

ACCEPT all of your duties as divine commands. — *Immanuel Kant*

DUTY is the demand of the passing hour. — *Geothe*

ANYONE can carry his burden, however hard, until nightfall. Anyone can do his work, however hard, for one day.
— *Robert Louis Stevenson*

EARLY RISERS

ONLY a few men live to an old age, and fewer still become successful who are not early risers. — *Benjamin Franklin*

I AM glad most folks don't get up very early. If they did, they'd rob chaps like me of the best part of the day. As it is, early morning is the time I like best. You can cross the road without looking right or left. You don't have a lot of noises that get on your nerves. If there's a grand sunrise you can stand and look at it without everybody thinking you're crazy. Even in the middle of the city you can hear sparrows chirping fit to bust. I like mornings, and it may be selfish but I like having them all to myself. — *Alfred A. Montapert*

ECONOMIST

IF you laid all the economists in our country end to end, they would point in every direction. — *Washington Dragon*

EDUCATION

THE true purpose of education is the harmonious development of all our faculties ... and the first object of any learning is that it should serve us in the future. — *Alfred A. Montapert*

A MAN who has never gone to school may steal from a freight car; but if he has a university education, he may steal the railroad. — *Theodore Roosevelt*

THE best conceivable graduate of the best conceivable school needs adult education as badly as the worst. As far as genuine education is concerned, there are no finishing schools. — *Mortimer J. Adler*

IT is time that we had uncommon schools, that we did not leave off our education when we begin to be men and women. It is time that villages were universities, and their elder inhabitants the fellows of universities, with leisure — if they are, indeed, so well off — to pursue liberal studies the rest of their lives. — *Henry David Thoreau*

I HAVE no technical and no University education, and have just had to pick up a few things as I went along. — *Sir Winston Churchill*

SOME are so very studious of learning what was done by the ancients that they know not how to live with the moderns. — *William Penn*

THE question to be asked at the end of any educational step is not what has the person learned, but what has the person BECOME? To become the WHOLE PERSON you are capable of becoming is the ULTIMATE IN LIFE. — *Alfred A. Montapert*

EDUCATION is turning things over in the mind. — *Robert Frost*

THE best service a book, a sermon, or a lecture can render you is not merely to impart truth, but to make you think it out for yourself.
— *A. P. Gouthey*

EDUCATION commences at the mother's knee, and every word spoken within the hearing of little children tends toward formation of character. — *H. Ballou*

EDUCATE men without religion and you make them but clever devils.

— *Arthur Wellesley*
Duke of Wellington

EDUCATION is leading human souls to what is best, and making what is best of them. The training which makes men happiest in themselves also makes them most serviceable to others. — *John Ruskin*

NATURE and books belong to the eyes that see them.
— *Ralph Waldo Emerson*

MY greatest complaint of education is that it is so loaded with material you never move in the spirit again. — *Robert Frost*

EVERY man should have a college education in order to show him how little the thing is really worth. — *Elbert Hubbard*

NATURAL ability without education has more often raised a man to glory and virtue than education without natural ability. — *Cicero*

NATIVE ability without education is like a tree without fruit.
— *Aristippus*

EDUCATION without God gives one greater capacity to get into trouble. — *Alfred A. Montapert*

EDUCATION

THE aim of education should be the achievement of results that the STUDENT requires by reason of his human nature, and not the production of effects that the EDUCATOR believes should be had.

— *Alexis Carrel*

EVERYONE receives two educations: the education which he gets from others, and the education which he gives to himself. Of the two the second is the more important. — *Edward Gibbon*

THE mark of an educated man is the ability to make a reasoned guess on the basis of insufficient information. — *Abbott L. Lowell*

EDUCATION is not preparation for life; Education is life itself.

— *John Dewey*

ELOQUENCE

ELOQUENCE is the power to translate a truth into language perfectly intelligible to the person to whom you speak.

— *Ralph Waldo Emerson*

ENCOURAGEMENT

THOSE whom you can make like themselves better will, I promise you, like you very well. — *Lord Chesterfield*

YOU can't stop people from thinking . . . but you can start them.

— *Frank A. Dusch*

ENCOURAGEMENT is oxygen to the soul! — *Anonymous*

NO MAN is great in and of himself; he must touch the lives of other great beings who will inspire him, lift him, and push him forward.

— *Alfred A. Montapert*

END

THERE is no end in nature, but every end is a beginning.
— Ralph Waldo Emerson

TO BE what we are, and to become what we are capable of becoming, is the only end of life.   *— Robert Lewis Stevenson*

ENDURANCE

A MAN can stand a lot as long as he can stand himself. *— Alex Munthe*

SUCCESS seems to be largely a matter of hanging on after others have let go.   *— William Feather*

ENEMY

NOTHING is so dangerous as an ignorant friend; a wise enemy is much better.   *— Jean de La Fontaine*

IT is my rule, from experience, to remember my friend may become my enemy, and my enemy my friend.   *— Sophocles*

ENTHUSIASM

ENTHUSIASM is to personality what steam is to a locomotive . . . the power that produces action.   *— Alfred A. Montapert*

EVERY product of genius must be the production of enthusiasm.
— Benjamin Disraeli

ENTHUSIASM is a volcano on whose top never grows the grass of hesitation.   *— Kahlil Gibran*

ENVIRONMENT

THE environment you fashion out of your thoughts, your beliefs, your ideals, your philosophy, is the only climate you will ever live in.
— *Alfred A. Montapert*

EPITAPH

WHAT we gave, we have; what we spent, we had; what we left, we lost.
— *Earl of Devon, Epitaph*

ESSENTIALS

ESSENTIAL things are the easiest things of all to overlook, neglect, or relegate to second place. The reason probably is, other things are nearer to us and therefore seem more real. To keep first things in first place is the fine art of Christian living.
— *Alfred A. Montapert*

THE man that is wise will gain the knowledge of Him.
— *Frederick K. C. Price*

ETERNITY

ETERNITY is written in the skies.
— *Young*

GOD has set eternity in our hearts, Solomon tells us. We are built for two worlds. It is impossible for any of us to fully live within the narrow confines of this materialistic present. We were built not for fifty years but for fifty million.
— *Alfred A. Montapert*

I FEEL the flame of eternity in my soul.
— *Helen Keller*

ETHICS

THE greatest need in ethics is the impartial and unselfish will to do right. — *Borden Parker Bowne*

ONLY that entirely universal and absolute purposiveness with regard to the maintenance and enhancement of life, which is the aim of reverence for life, is really ethical. — *Albert Schweitzer*

EVIL

GOD makes all things good; man meddles with them and they become evil. — *Jean Jacques Rousseau*

THERE are a thousand hacking at the branches of evil . . . to one who is striking at the root. — *Henry David Thoreau*

EVIL is that which is opposed to life, to its multiplication or to its spiritual development. — *Alexis Carrel*

BETTER be poor than wicked. — *Proverb*

GOOD EXAMPLE

SO ACT that your principle of action might safely be made a law for the whole world. — *Immanuel Kant*

LET him who wants to move and convince others be first moved and convinced himself. — *Thomas Carlyle*

FEW things are harder to put up with than the annoyance of a good example. — *Mark Twain*

A GOOD example is a lesson anyone can read. — *Anonymous*

EXCESS

AS many suffer from too much as too little. — *Christian N. Bovee*

ALL excess is ill ... but drunkenness is of the worst sort. It spoils health, dismounts the mind, and unmans men. It reveals secrets, and is quarrelsome, lascivious, impudent, dangerous and bad.

— *Thomas Jefferson*

HE who undertakes too much seldom succeeds. — *Dutch Proverb*

EXECUTIVE

THE most valuable executive is one who is training somebody to be a better man than he is. — *Robert G. Ingersoll*

AN executive is a person who gets his hair cut on company time.

— *Anonymous*

EXERCISE

I LIKE long walks, especially when they are taken by people who annoy me. — *Fred Allen*

THERE is nothing better for the inside of a man than the outside of a horse. — *Oliver Cromwell*

NOTHING beats walking ... at least an hour every day. Make walking an hour or two a day so habitual it becomes second nature to you ... something you must have ... as important to you as eating and sleeping! — *Dr. Lawrence E. Lamb*

EXPECTATIONS

THERE is probably but one answer to the question, "What do we get out of life?" And that is, we get out of life exactly what we put into it, but we get that back in great abundance. — *William Ross*

SOMETHING great and wonderful is happening today, and I am part of it. — *Dr. Robert Scott*

WHAT we anticipate seldom occurs; but what we least expect generally happens. — *Benjamin Disraeli*

IF you do not expect the unexpected, you will not find it.
 — *Heraclitus*

WHATEVER other habits we form, let us form the habit of expectancy. An expectant frame of mind attracts what we expect. — *Unknown*

EXPECT a miracle! — *Oral Roberts*

EXPERIENCE

IF you take all the experience and judgment of men over fifty out of the world, there wouldn't be enough left to run it. — *Henry Ford*

THE more extensive a man's knowledge of what has been done, the greater will be his power of knowing what to do. — *Benjamin Disraeli*

AN OUNCE of practice is worth a pound of preaching. — *Anonymous*

IT has done me good to be somewhat parched by the heat and drenched by the rain of life. — *Henry Wadsworth Longfellow*

THE years teach much which the days never know.
 — *Ralph Waldo Emerson*

EXPERIENCE

EXPERIENCE is a good school, but the fees are high.

— Heinrich Heine

A WISE man can learn from another man's experience. A fool cannot learn even from his own. *— Will Durant*

LIVING will teach you how to live, better than preacher or book.

— Johann W. Goethe

EXPERIENCE is not what happens to you, it is what you do with what happens to you. *— Aldous Huxley*

EXPERIENCE is your working capital. *— Anonymous*

THE knowledge of the world is only to be acquired in the world.

— Earl of Chesterfield

WE must use and honor the wisdom of the ages and preserve for the modern world some part of mankind's heritage of dreams, hopes and aspirations. We must learn from the past. *— Alfred A. Montapert*

EXPLANATION

NEVER explain ... your friends do not need it and your enemies will not believe you anyway. *— Elbert G. Hubbard*

FAILURE

MEN don't plan to fail, they fail to plan. *— Alfred A. Montapert*

FAILURE

OUR greatest glory consists not in never falling, but in rising every time we fall.   — *Ralph Waldo Emerson*

FAILURE is not falling down, but staying down.   — *Mary Pickford*

TO DO nothing is in every man's power.   — *Samuel Johnson*

TO FAIL with God in a cause which will ultimately succeed is better than to succeed in a cause that will ultimately fail.
                                            — *Alfred A. Montapert*

FAITH

FAITH is the MIGHTY POWER OF GOD. It is the fire in the heart, and without it you are nothing. FAITH and BELIEF . . . the unbeatable combination for LIFE . . . HEALTH . . . WEALTH . . . and HAPPINESS.   — *Alfred A. Montapert*

FAITH makes us, and not we it, and faith makes its own forms.
                                            — *Ralph Waldo Emerson*

FAITH is, above all, openness . . . an act of trust in the unknown.
                                            — *Alan Watts*

HAVE courage for the great sorrows of life, and patience for the small ones. And when you have accomplished your daily tasks, go to sleep in peace. God is awake.   — *Victor Hugo*

FAITH in man is a duty as well as faith in God. When that faith ceases, society ceases with it.   — *John Stuart Blackie*

NOW FAITH is the substance of things hoped for, the evidence of things not seen.   — *Hebrews 11:1*

FAITH

FAITH is a Positive, Dynamic Force that gives Meaning and Power to the Business of Life. "According to your FAITH be it done unto you" . . . according to both the amount and quality of it.

— Alfred A. Montapert

FAITH is a knowledge within the heart, beyond the reach of proof.

— Kahlil Gibran

A MAN consists of the faith that is in him. Whatever his faith is, he is.

— Bhagavad-Gita

FEW people realize what a substantial thing faith is.

— Henry Ford

FAITH is a gift that you have always owned. It is another of the great gifts that the Divine Plan has placed within your grasp. It is a gift that can carry you successfully on any road you choose.

— Walter M. Germain

AND whoso trusteth in the Lord, happy is he.   *— Proverbs 16:20*

FAITH is believing before receiving. If a thing cannot be done . . . only faith can do it. Faith is not contrary to reason . . . but rather, reason grown courageous.   *— Alfred A. Montapert*

TALK unbelief, and you will have unbelief; but talk faith, and you will have faith. According to the seed sown will be the harvest.

— Ellen G. White

FEAR knocked. Faith opened the door.   *— Anonymous*

FAITH is the great, positive, affirmative attitude of mind, and it is powerful because it is in agreement with God.

— Ernest Holmes

CALMNESS is only another word for confidence. And confidence is faith in action.
— *Anonymous*

CAST all your cares on God; that anchor holds.
— *Alfred Lord Tennyson*

A MAN of courage is also full of faith.
— *Cicero*

THE only limit to our realization of tomorrow will be our doubts of today. Let us move forward with strong and active faith.
— *Franklin D. Roosevelt*

FAME

POPULARITY? It is glory's small change.
— *Victor Hugo*

ALL the fame I look for in this life is to have lived it quietly.
— *Michel de Montaigne*

FAMILY

THE BOND that links your true family is not one of blood, but of respect and joy in each other's life.
— *Richard Bach*

FATE

FATE with impartial hand turns out the doom of high and low; her capacious urn is constantly shaking out the names of all mankind.
— *Horace*

MAN is man, and master of his fate; what you wish to be, that you are, for such is the force of our will, joined to the Supreme, that whatever we wish to be, seriously, and with true intention, that we become.
— *Jean Paul Richter*

FAULTS

WE keep the faults of others before our eyes; our own behind our backs.
— *Seneca*

MAN'S chief fault is that he has so many small ones.
— *Jean Paul Richter*

BEFORE you correct your faults, you must face them.
— *Walter M. Germain*

FAVORS

TO ACCEPT a favor is to forfeit liberty.   — *Louise H. Leber*

HE receives most favors who knows how to return them.
— *Publilius Syrus*

FAVORS cease to be favors when there are conditions attached to them.
— *Thornton Wilder*

FEAR

WHEN you are established in righteousness ... you will overcome fear.
— *Alfred A. Montapert*

THE only thing we have to fear ... is fear itself.
— *Franklin D. Roosevelt*

PERFECT love casteth out fear.   — *1 John 4:18*

FEAR is the wrong use of imagination. It is anticipating the worst, not the best that can happen.
— *Anonymous*

THE first duty of man is that of subduing fear. We must get rid of fear; we cannot act at all till then. A man's acts are slavish, not true but specious; his very thoughts are false, he thinks too as a slave and coward, until he has got fear under his feet.

— *Thomas Carlyle*

FEELINGS

THE ennobling difference between one man and another is that one feels more than another. — *John Ruskin*

IF I can't feel a theme, I can't make a film anyone else will feel. I can't laugh at intellectual humor. I'm just corny enough to like to have a story hit me over the heart. — *Walt Disney*

FIDELITY

FIDELITY bought with money is overcome by money. — *Seneca*

FLATTERY

FLATTERY is all right . . . if you don't inhale. — *Adlai E. Stevenson*

IMITATION is the sincerest form of flattery. — *Charles Caleb Colton*

FOLLY

FOLLY is the one evil for which there is no remedy.

— *Spanish Saying*

EVEN God cannot save a fool from his folly. — *Alfred A. Montapert*

FOOL

LET us be thankful for the fools. But for them the rest of us could not succeed.

— *Mark Twain*

HE WHO asks a question may be a fool for five minutes. But he who never asks a question remains a fool forever.

— *Tom J. Connelly*

A FOOL and her money are soon courted.

— *Helen Rowland*

IT is sometimes necessary to play the fool to avoid being deceived by clever men.

— *La Rochefoucauld*

FOOLS take to themselves the respect that is given to their office.

— *Aesop*

FORGIVENESS

HUMANITY is never so beautiful as when praying for forgiveness, or else forgiving another.

— *Jean Paul Richter*

WHEN a deep injury is done to us, we never recover until we forgive.

— *Alan Paton*

HE who forgives ... ends the quarrel!

— *Anonymous*

AND when ye stand praying, forgive, if you have ought against any; that your Father also which is in heaven may forgive you your trespasses. But if ye do not forgive, neither will your Father which is in heaven forgive your trespasses.

— *Mark 11:25*

FORCE

I AM told that nothing that we do on earth, and nothing that we make on earth, is in as great abundance as force. We now have 30,000 pounds of destructive force, TNT equivalent, available for every human being on earth. We don't have 30,000 pounds of food or medicine or art or books or any of the things that ennoble life, but we have 30,000 pounds of instant force for every human being on earth.
— *Norman Cousins*

FORTUNE

THERE is a tide in the affairs of men which, taken at the flood, leads on to fortune; omitted, all the voyage of their life is bound in shallows and in miseries.
— *William Shakespeare*

WHEN fortune smiles, embrace her.
— *Anonymous*

A MAN can hardly be said to have made a fortune if he does not know how to enjoy it.
— *Vauvenargues*

THE mold of a man's fortune is in his hands.
— *Francis Bacon*

THE BEST fortune that can fall to a man is that which corrects his defects and makes up for his failings.
— *Goethe*

FOUNDATION

I RESPECT the man who knows distinctly what he wishes. The greater part of all the mischief in the world arises from the fact that men do not sufficiently understand their own aims. They have undertaken to build a tower, and spend no more on the foundation than would be necessary to erect a hut.
— *Goethe*

FOUNDATION

BUILD castles in the air, but put foundations under them.
— *Henry David Thoreau*

FOR other foundation can no man lay than that is laid, which is Jesus Christ.
— *1 Corinthians 3:11*

FREEDOM

HAVE we too much freedom? Have we so long ridiculed authority in the family, discipline in education, rules in art, decency in conduct, and law in the state, that our liberation has brought us close to chaos in the family and the school, in morals, arts, ideas and government? We forgot to make ourselves intelligent when we made ourselves free.
— *Will Durant*

THE founders of the Republic knew, as did Pericles, that if the secret of happiness was freedom, "the secret of freedom is a brave heart."
— *Felix Frankfurter*

FREEDOM is not a question of doing as we like but doing as we ought.
— *Anonymous*

A HUMAN being is always a prisoner of something. The only freedom is within ourselves.
— *Alfred A. Montapert*

SO FAR as man thinks, he is free.
— *Ralph Waldo Emerson*

THE only true law is that which leads to freedom. There is no other.
— *Richard Bach*

CHOOSING freedom, a man can stand up. A man can believe at his own risk and fight for his faith in his own power.
— *Horace Mayer Kallen*

HE is free who carries the slave's burden with patience.
— *Kahlil Gibran*

THERE are two good things in life . . . freedom of thought . . . and freedom of action. — *W. Somerset Maugham*

I BELIEVE each individual is naturally entitled to do as he pleases with himself and the fruits of his labor, so far as it in no wise interferes with any other man's rights. — *Abraham Lincoln*

TRUE freedom is not merely political, but must also be economic and spiritual. Only then can man grow and fulfill his destiny.
— *Jawaharlal Nehru*

IT is not good to be too free. It is not good to have everything one wants. — *Blaise Pascal*

GOD is no dictator. He leaves us the freedom to master ourselves.
— *Mahatma Gandhi*

FRESH AIR

FRESH AIR gives you sixty percent of your energy. Love the open air. When you are out-of-doors, the touch of earth and the breath of the fresh air gives you fresh life and energy. Men, like trees, live in great part on fresh air. — *Alfred A. Montapert*

FRICTION

A DIAMOND cannot be polished without grinding, nor a man perfected without hardship and trials. — *Anonymous*

WITHOUT lubrication, machinery is impossible.— *Alfred A. Montapert*

FRIEND

OUR chief want in life is somebody who shall make us do what we can. This is the service of a friend.   — *Ralph Waldo Emerson*

A FRIEND is a person:
    –With whom you can be sincere.
    –To whom you do not need to explain yourself.
    –To whom you never need defend yourself.
    –On whom you can depend whether present or absent.
    –With whom you never need pretend.
    –To whom you can reveal yourself without fear of betrayal.
    –Who does not feel he owns you because you are his friend.
    –Who will not selfishly use you because he has your confidence.
I would have such a friend . . . and I would be such a friend.
                                                — *Alfred A. Montapert*

A REAL friend is one who walks in when the rest of the world walks out.   — *Walter Winchell*

MAKE friends and you will make greater progress. The way to make a true friend is to be one. Friendship implies loyalty, esteem, cordiality, sympathy, affection, readiness to aid, to help, to stick, to fight for. Friends are essential to success; they are still more essential to happiness. To win place, power, honor and happiness, begin by assiduously and unselfishly winning friends.   — *B.C. Forbes*

WITHOUT a friend, the world is but a wilderness. A man may have a thousand intimate acquaintances and not a friend among them all. If you have one true friend, think yourself rich.   — *Noah Webster*

NO MAN can be happy without a friend, nor be sure of his friend until he is unhappy.   — *Thomas Fuller*

SO long as you are prosperous you will reckon many friends; if fortune frowns on you, you will be alone. — *Ovid*

A WORD from a friend is doubly enjoyable in dark days. — *Goethe*

BE slow in choosing a friend, but slower in changing him.
— *Scottish Proverb*

IT is prosperity that gives us friends; adversity that proves them.
— *French Saying*

HAPPY is the man who has a friend who knows all about him . . . and yet remains his friend. — *A.P. Gouthey*

THE most I can do for my friend is simply to be his friend.
— *Henry David Thoreau*

TRUE happiness consists not in the miltitude of friends, but in their worth and value. — *Ben Johnson*

WE are all travellers in the wilderness of this world, and the best that we find in our travels is an honest friend.
— *Robert Louis Stevenson*

LET your friends be the friends of your deliberate choice.
— *Baltasar Gracian*

ALL men's friend, no man's friend. — *John Wodroephe*

BE gracious to all men, but choose the best to be your friends.
— *Socrates*

YOUR friends will know you better in the first minute you meet than your acquaintances will know you in a thousand years.
— *Richard Bach*

FRIENDSHIP

AND let there be no purpose in friendship save the deepening of the spirit.

— Kahlil Gibran

FALSE friendship, like the ivy, decays and ruins the wall it embraces; but true friendship gives new life and animation to the object of support.

— Richard E. Burton

IF a man does not make new acquaintance as he advances through life, he will soon find himself left alone. A man, Sir, should keep his friendship in constant repair.

— Samuel Johnson

FRIENDSHIP is the only thing in the world concerning the usefulness of which all men are agreed.

— Cicero

NOTHING so fortifies a friendship as a belief on the part of one friend that he is superior to the other.

— Honore de Balzac

OH, the comfort, the inexpressible comfort of feeling safe with a person, having neither to weigh thoughts nor measure words, but pouring all right out just as they are, chaff and grain together, certain that a faithful hand will take and sift them, keep what is worth keeping, and with a breath of comfort, blow the rest away.

— Charles Gow

THE glory of friendship . . . is the inspiration that comes to one when he discovers that someone else believes in him and is willing to trust him.

— Ralph Waldo Emerson

FRIENDSHIP can be discussed for a hundred years, but the experience of one good friend will transform a theory into a fact.

— Alfred A. Montapert

ONE of the best ways to keep friendship is to return it. — *Anonymous*

FRIENDSHIP flourishes at the fountain of forgiveness.
— *William A. Ward*

DON'T flatter yourself that friendship authorizes you to say disagreeable things to your intimates. The nearer you come into relation with a person, the more necessary does tact and courtesy become. Except in cases of necessity, which are rare, leave your friend to learn unpleasant things from his enemies; they are ready enough to tell them. — *Oliver Wendell Holmes*

FULFILLMENT

BE not contented with little; he who brings to the springs of life an empty jar will return with two full ones. — *Kahlil Gibran*

A MAN is relieved and gay when he has put his heart into his work and done his best; but that he has done otherwise shall give him no peace. — *Ralph Waldo Emerson*

MY first business is to so live that at least a few will thank God that I lived when my little day is done. — *Alfred A. Montapert*

GROWING spiritually, we discover to our joy that the deepest needs of our lives can be fulfilled, that the longing person can find an answer to his longing. The deep desire for meaning, for fulfillment, for wholeness, can be satisfied. The water of life is set flowing by God and, freely offered, gives new life to all who receive it.
— *Norman Vincent Peale*

FULFILLMENT is ... to incorporate the Word of the Eternal God in my complete being. — *Alfred A. Montapert*

FUTURE

MY interest is in the future because I am going to spend the rest of my life there.   — *Charles F. Kettering*

STUDY the past if you would define the future.   — *Confucius*

THE best thing about the future is that it comes only one day at a time.   — *Anonymous*

THE future hides in it gladness and sorrow.   — *Goethe*

I KNOW no way of judging the future but by the past.
                                                — *Patrick Henry*

THE PAST, no matter how great or good, will not sustain the future. That truth goes double. A great and good past but obligates one to make a greater and better future. That, in a nutshell, is my hope and dream and vision.   — *Alfred A. Montapert*

THE future is a world limited by ourselves.   — *Maurice Maeterlinck*

INVENTOR, poet, prophet ... all belong to the same class, all are seers.   — *Anonymous*

MAN is born a long way from himself. He needs to see the end toward which he moves. The immediate must be absorbed by the future. The measure of his strength must be revealed by a vision of his highest faculty. He must see the unseen and work in the realm of the invisible. Happy is the man who learns that the present is but the challenge of his future.   — *Alfred A. Montapert*

GAIN

LET this be an example for the acquisition of all knowledge, virtue and riches: By the fall of drops of water, by degrees, a pot is filled.
                                                — *Hitopeseda*

GENEROSITY

THE size of a person's world is the size of his heart.
— *Alfred A. Montapert*

GENEROSITY does not reject and therefore will not be rejected.
— *Lao Tzu*

GENIUS

GENIUS is eternal patience. — *Michelangelo*

PLATO has well said, "Genius is work, plus more work." Greatness does not fly to the land of achievement on the magic carpet of wishful thinking. — *Alfred A. Montapert*

MEN give me some credit for genius. All the genius I have lies in this: When I have a subject in hand, I study it profoundly. Day and night it is before me. I explore it in all its bearings. My mind becomes pervaded with it. Then the effort which I make the people are pleased to call the fruit of genius. It is the fruit of labor and thought. — *Alexander Hamilton*

AS a rule, adversity reveals genius and prosperity conceals it.
— *Horace*

GENIUS is childhood recaptured. — *Baudelaire*

WHEN a true genius appears in the world, you may know him by this sign . . . that the dunces are all in a confederacy against him.
— *Jonathan Swift*

GENTLEMAN

A GENTLEMAN is a man who can disagree without being disagreeable.
— *Anonymous*

GENTLENESS

ONLY people who possess firmness can possess genuine gentleness.
— *La Rochefoucauld*

GENTLENESS is a divine trait; nothing is so strong as gentleness and nothing is so gentle as real strength.
— *Unknown*

GIFT

THE best gift to your enemy is forgiveness; an opponent, tolerance; a friend, your heart; your child, a good example; to a father, deference; to your mother, conduct that will make her proud of you; to yourself, respect; to all men, charity.
— *Francis M. Balfour*

A GIFT much expected is rather paid than given.
— *William D. Montapert*

THE only true gift is a portion of thyself.
— *Ralph Waldo Emerson*

GIVE/GIVING

WHAT can I give Him, Poor as I am?
If I were a shepherd, I would bring a lamb,
If I were a wise man, I would do my part,
Yet what can I give Him? Give Him my heart.

— *Christina Rossetti*

YOU get the best out of others, when you give the best of yourself.
— *Harvey Firestone*

EVERYONE is a channel through whom God sees, thinks, works, and acts. We are continually receiving. We cannot give before we receive, but if we do not GIVE after we receive, we obstruct or close the channel. — *Alfred A. Montapert*

LET us then give as we have received. Life will always strike the balance in our favor. Give as freely as we are able, we will never give back more than a fraction of what we receive. — *James D. Freeman*

MAKE it a rule, and pray God to help you keep it, never, if possible, to lie down at night without being able to say, "I have made one human being at least a little wiser, a little happier or a little better this day." — *Charles Kingsley*

GIVE, and it shall be given unto you; good measure, pressed down, and shaken together, and running over, shall men give into your bosom. For with the same measure that ye mete withal it shall be measured to you again. — *Luke 6:38*

ONLY as we give with no thought of getting do we really get.
— *Alfred A. Montapert*

GIVING is vital to spiritual growth. To give without thought of gain, to help without expectation of personal benefit, is the ultimate in loving concern. Whenever a good thought is spoken, somewhere is an answering response. No kindly act is performed that does not return to bless. Give yourself and find yourself. Your own will come to you. — *Norman Vincent Peale*

IT is foolish to wait for your ship to come in unless you have sent one out. — *Alfred A. Montapert*

GO FORWARD

THAT which I have done, I now proceed to forget. It is of the past. My role is to search always for the now. Do not speak of that which I have already done.
— *Alexis Carrel*

THE BUSINESS of life is to go forwards.
— *Samuel Johnson*

LOOK ahead or you will fall behind.
— *Hanford L. Gordon*

SOMETIMES it is a necessity and an advantage to burn one's bridges behind. When one's avenue of retreat is cut off, there is only one way to go . . . FORWARD!
— *Unknown*

GOALS

BITE off more than you can chew, then chew it. Plan more than you can do . . . then do it.
— *Alfred A. Montapert*

ALL men seek one goal: Success or happiness. The only way to achieve true success is to express yourself completely in service to society. First, have a definite, clear, practical ideal . . . a goal, an objective. Second, have the necessary means to achieve your ends . . . wisdom, money, materials and methods. Third, adjust all your means to that end.
— *Aristotle*

NO wind blows in favor of a ship with no port of destination.
— *Michel de Montaigne*

WHEN you determine what you want, you have made the most important decision of your life. You have to know what you want in order to attain it.
— *Douglas Lurtan*

THE Greatest Goal of Life is to know GOD, and JESUS CHRIST, which is Eternal Life. — *Alfred A. Montapert*

GOALS are as essential to success as air is to life. — *David Schwartz*

MAY you always have another mountain to conquer. Then you will know that you are truly alive! — *Robert Schuller*

LIFE'S greatest goals cannot be reached without a pattern or plan of procedure. No better or more ideal pattern could be conceived than that of Jesus. There can be no greater objective than to do God's will. Keep in line with the WORD OF GOD. — *Alfred A. Montapert*

I FEEL you set a goal to be the best and then you work every waking hour of each day trying to achieve that goal. — *Don Shula*

REACH for nothing . . . and you get it. — *Anonymous*

IN life, the FIRST thing you must do is decide what you really want. Weigh the costs and the results. Are the results worthy of the costs? Then make up your mind completely . . . and go after your goals with all your might. — *Alfred A. Montapert*

GOD

THE heavens declare the glory of God; and the firmament showeth His handiwork. — *Psalm 19:1*

GOD has two dwellings: one in heaven and the other in a meek and thankful heart. — *Anonymous*

WE, each of us, are a distinct part of the essence of God and contain a certain part of Him in ourselves. — *Epictetus*

GOD

WHEN we behold the Godness in all things, when we embrace the universe in its entirety, we are actually realizing God as the incomparable element in the universe. — *Randolph Schmelig*

IN HIM we live, and move, and have our being. — *Acts 17:28*

UNLESS we are governed by God, we will be ruled by tyrants. — *William Penn*

HOW dear, how soothing to man, arises the idea of God, peopling the lonely place, effacing the scars of our mistakes and disappointments. — *Ralph Waldo Emerson*

GOD'S language is the language of the heart . . . not of the tongue. — *Alfred A. Montapert*

THE longer I live, the more convincing proofs I see of this truth, that God governs in the affairs of man; and if a sparrow cannot fall to the ground without His notice, is it probable that an empire can rise without His aid? — *Benjamin Franklin*

GOD has placed a torch in your hearts that glows with knowledge and beauty; it is a sin to extinguish that torch and bury it in the ashes. — *Kahlil Gibran*

NONE of us is sufficient unto himself. So say the Scriptures. So says experience and observation. Not even God is independent of cooperation. We must labor together with Him or His best-laid plans cannot achieve their full purpose. So, you and I must give our best in order to achieve the full purpose of God. — *Alfred A. Montapert*

GOD is Big enough to rule HIS mighty Universe, Yet small enough to live within my heart! — *Beverly A. Reed*

GOD

NO nation can be ruled without God. No nation can be governed without God. No nation can grow without God. The finite will fail without FAITH in the INFINITE. *— Napoleon Bonaparte*

IF God did not exist, it would be necessary to invent Him. *— Voltaire*

LET shallow minds reject and ridicule as they may, the fact remains there is no explanation of the Universe, nor of man, apart from the creative genius of God. *— Alfred A. Montapert*

THE sun with all its planets moving around it can ripen the smallest bunch of grapes as if it had nothing else to do. Why then should I doubt HIS power? *— Galileo*

IN all thy ways acknowledge Him, and He shall direct thy paths. *— Proverbs 3:6*

EVERYONE who is seriously involved in the pursuit of science becomes convinced that a spirit is manifest in the laws of the universe . . . a spirit vastly superior to that of man, and one in the face of which we with our modest powers must feel humble. *— Albert Einstein*

BUT it is written, Eye hath not seen, nor ear heard, neither have entered into the heart of man, the things which God hath prepared for them that love Him. *— I Corinthians 2:9*

GOD is a generous giver, wanting us to have every good thing. Our good awaits us, an abundant good. Spiritual growth teaches us to believe in that good, to be a delighted receiver of God's goodness. He offers happiness. Take it. He offers peace. Take it. He offers renewal of body, mind and spirit. Even when old, you can feel youthfulness of spirit. *— Norman Vincent Peale*

GOD AND MAN

THERE is no such thing as highest and best living . . . except as we walk on the level of God's thinking, and God's saying. It is not in ANY man to direct his own way. If we keep up the egotistical assumption that we are wholly sufficient unto ourselves, we end up bankrupt. — *Alfred A. Montapert*

MAN'S discovery of God is the most wonderful story ever told, and whether he admits it to himself or not, his need for God is ever-present. — *Cecil B. DeMille*

THE things which are impossible with men are possible with God.
— *Anonymous*

AS is the MAN, so is his GOD. — *Goethe*

THE most ennobling experience in life is the awareness that one is an instrument of deity being used to further His purpose on the earth. — *A.P. Gouthey*

MAN is capable of realizing that he is a creature of God. It is this realization which makes him great. — *Alfred A. Montapert*

GOD is at the center of Man. — *Friedrich Von Schiller*

HE who knows God, worships Him. — *Seneca*

DON'T give me so much credit for my work. The credit is not all mine. I mean only that I am merely the instrument through which a Supreme Intelligence carries on His work.
— *Thomas Alva Edison*

WHEN man reaches his extremity, God gets His opportunity.
— *Anonymous*

HAVE I developed my full potential? I have, if MY FAITH IS STRONG ... it is the Father within me that doeth the work.
— *Alfred A. Montapert*

KNOW then thyself, presume not God to scan.
The proper study of mankind is man.
Seek thou within: seek not for God above!
The proper name for God in man is Love.   — *Alexander Pope*

LET none turn over books or scan the stars in quest of God who sees Him not in man.   — *Johann K. Lavater*

WE know that all spiritual being is in man.   — *Ralph Waldo Emerson*

GOD, who placed me here, will do what he pleases with me hereafter, and He knows best what to do.   — *Alfred A. Montapert*

THE greatest minds who have ever lived have believed in this relationship of God and Man, and there is nothing in science that refutes it; rather, science is confirming it.   — *Ernest Holmes*

HERE you have two forces working, the forces of the HIGHEST POWER, GOD, plus the Natural forces and skills of Man. This is the unbeatable combination.   — *Alfred A. Montapert*

MAN must build on God alone.   — *Meister Eckhart*

THERE is enough of God in the worst man to prove there is a God.
— *Anonymous*

STUDY to obey GOD'S WORD in everything, and keep in HIS WILL and HIS WAY. This is your DUTY and your WISDOM. This is the TRUTH and the SECRET of genuine JOY and SOLID PEACE within. "I am the WAY, the TRUTH, and the LIFE."
— *Alfred A. Montapert*

GOOD DEEDS

HOW far that little candle throws his beam! So shines a good deed in a naughty world.   — *William Shakespeare*

A GOOD man makes no noise over a good deed, but passes on to another as a vine to bear grapes again in season.   — *Marcus Aurelius*

IT is one of the most beautiful compensations of this life that no man can sincerely try to help another without helping himself.
     — *Ralph Waldo Emerson*

ONE day, in my despair, I threw myself into a chair in the consulting room and groaned out: "What a blockhead I was to come out here to doctor savages like these!" Whereupon Joseph quietly remarked: "Yes, Doctor, here on earth you are a great blockhead, but not in heaven."   — *Albert Schweitzer*

GOODNESS

THE great end of LIFE is GOODNESS. Life is a battle . . . a test . . . and a reward. When you combine GOLD and GOODNESS, you have reached the highest plateau of living.   — *Alfred A. Montapert*

THE good life is one inspired by love and guided by knowledge.
     — *Bertrand Russell*

ONE must strain to hear Goodness, for it is seldom vocal. It is only Evil that sounds its voice.   — *Anonymous*

LITTLE progress can be made by merely attempting to repress what is evil; our great hope lies in developing what is good.
     — *Calvin Coolidge*

THE main source of our wealth is GOODNESS. The AFFECTIONS and the GENEROUS QUALITIES that God admires in a world full of Greed.   — *Alfred A. Montapert*

GOSSIPS

THE person who gossips to you will gossip about you.

— *Old Adage*

THERE is so much good in the worst of us, and so much bad in the best of us, that it behooves all of us not to talk about the rest of us.

— *Robert Louis Stevenson*

GOVERNMENT

REMEMBER that this government is the best in the world. Improve it, but guard it well, and don't lean too heavily on it.

— *Bernard Baruch*

WHAT government is the best? That which teaches us to govern ourselves.

— *Goethe*

THERE is a myth that government can do the job cheaper because it does not have to make a profit. The records show that anything the government does will cost ten times more than private enterprise.

— *Alfred A. Montapert*

THE function of Government must be to favor no small group at the expense of its duty to protect the rights of personal freedom and of private property of all its citizens.

— *Franklin D. Roosevelt*

ALL forms of government destroy themselves by carrying their basic principle to excess ... The democracies become too free, in politics and economics, in morals, even in literature and art, until at last even the puppy dogs in our homes rise up on their hind legs and demand their rights. Disorder grows to such a point that a society will then abandon all its liberty to anyone who can restore order.

— *Plato (4th Century B.C.)*

GOVERNMENT

IT is time for the American people to look the government straight in the eye and say, "No more!" We will make the decisions about our lives. You protect us from foreign aggressors and domestic criminals, give us a stable currency and court of law, and we'll do the rest.
— *Gerald R. Ford*

POLITICIANS are full of unkept promises. They promise to build a bridge even where there is no river. — *Alfred A. Montapert*

THERE is no qualification for government, but Virtue and Wisdom.
— *Edmund Burke*

IT is the duty of Government to make it difficult for people to do wrong, easy to do right. — *William E. Gladstone*

THANK God we don't get all the government we pay for.
— *Will Rogers*

THE art of government consists in taking as much money as possible from one class of citizens to give to the other. — *Voltaire*

GRACE

WHAT is grace? It is the inspiration from on high; it is love; it is liberty. Grace is the spirit of law. This discovery of the spirit of law belongs to Saint Paul; and what he calls "grace" from a heavenly point of view, we, from an earthly point, call "righteousness."
— *Victor Hugo*

GRATITUDE

TO LOVE the good things of life is to be grateful for their existence.
— *Stella T. Mann*

GRATITUDE

WHILE praying for the moon and all lesser things, you may have better luck if you throw in a few words of gratitude for the blessings you now have. — *Alfred A. Montapert*

THERE are two kinds of gratitude . . . the sudden kind we feel for what we take, the larger kind we feel for what we give.
— *Edward Arlington Robinson*

GRATITUDE is not only a virtue it also is part of a practical philosophy of daily life. There is no wiser way of living than to remember every morning what Life has given us, and to lift up our thought in thankfulness for every bounty we possess. — *Ernest Holmes*

O LORD, give me a grateful heart! — *Alfred A. Montapert*

GREAT MAN

THE greatest man in history was the poorest. — *Ralph Waldo Emerson*

A GREAT man is he who can call together the most select company when it pleases him. — *Walter Savage Landor*

A GREAT thing can only be done by a great man, and he does it without effort. — *John Ruskin*

THE way of a superior man is threefold: Virtuous, he is free from anxieties; Wise, he is free from perplexities; Bold, he is free from fear. — *Confucius*

NAPOLEON was indeed a very great man, but he was also a very great actor. — *Duke of Wellington*

GREAT MAN

HOW much easier it is to please a great man than a little one.
— *George Bernard Shaw*

FOR the whole earth is the sepulchre of famous men and their story is not graven only on stone over their native earth but lives on far away without visible symbol woven into the stuff of other men's lives.
— *Pericles*

IT is not titles that honor men, but men that honor titles.
— *Niccolo Machiavelli*

GREAT men rejoice in adversity just as brave soldiers triumph in war.
— *Seneca*

DO not pride yourself on the few great men who, over the centuries, have been born on your earth . . . through no merit of yours. Reflect, rather, on how you have treated them at the time, and how you have followed their teachings.
— *Albert Einstein*

THE light of stars that were extinguished ages ago still reaches us. So it is with great men who died centuries ago, but still reach us with the radiations of their personality.
— *Kahlil Gibran*

GREATNESS

KEEP away from people who try to belittle your ambitions. Small people always do that, but the really great make you feel that you, too, can become great.
— *Mark Twain*

IT'S great to be great, but it's greater to be human.
— *Will Rogers*

I KNOW of no great man, except those who have rendered great services to the human race.
— *Voltaire*

BUT he that is greatest among you shall be your servant.

— *Matthew 23:11*

THE monument of a great man is NOT of Granite or Marble or Bronze. It consists of his GOODNESS, his DEEDS, his LOVE and COMPASSION.

— *Alfred A. Montapert*

THE first step to greatness is to be honest.

— *George Washington*

PEOPLE who know they are GOOD . . . have supreme CONFIDENCE in themselves. They have full consciousness of COMPETENCE. Their courage and CONVICTION come direct from the heart . . . and they RELAX to that degree which is necessary for TRUE GREATNESS. They KNOW they are WINNERS!

— *Alfred A. Montapert*

GREED

THE DARKEST hour in any man's life is when he sits down to plan how to get money without earning it.

— *Horace Greeley*

GRIEF

THE only thing grief has taught me is to know how shallow it is.

— *Ralph Waldo Emerson*

HAPPINESS is beneficial for the body but it is grief . . . that develops the powers of the mind.

— *Marcel Proust*

GROWTH

PILING up knowledge is as bad as piling up money indefinitely. You have to begin sometime to kick around what you know.— *Robert Frost*

GROWTH

LIFE is a continual process of remaking ourselves. — *Anonymous*

IT is only when men begin to worship that they begin to grow.
— *Calvin Coolidge*

YOU must know how to flower where God has sown you.
— *Jan de Hartog*

LIFE consists of melting illusions, correcting mistakes and replacing outworn clothing. But I remind myself there is no other way to grow.
— *A.P. Gouthey*

NEVER deny yourself life's experiences. Whether they are good or seem bad we should always learn, and hopefully grow from them.
— *Dani Unick*

STAY green and growing . . . for as soon as you are ripe you begin to rot. — *Ray Kroc*

YOUR intellectual and cultural growth did not end when you left school. Your curiosity about the human adventure remains lively. Your lifelong love of knowledge is demonstrated by the books you read. You learn up until your last breath. — *Alfred A. Montapert*

GUIDANCE

WHAT is the best guide to life? The Sermon on the Mount and the Ten Commandments. — *Bernard Baruch*

NEVER give a child a choice. Don't give him a choice of believing in God or not. He can start having choices when he goes to college.
— *Robert Frost*

O LORD, I know that the way of man is not in himself; it is not in man that walketh to direct his steps. — *Jeremiah 10:23*

GUILT

GUILT automatically produces fear . . . you can fool people . . . but you can't fool your own autonomic nervous system. — _Dr. Max Levine_

COMMIT a crime, and the earth is made of glass.
— _Ralph Waldo Emerson_

HABIT

HABIT is the best of servants, or the worst of masters.
— _Nathaniel Emmons_

YOUR life is governed by habit. Your habits are governed by you.
— _Walter M. Germain_

NOTHING so needs reforming as other people's habits.— _Mark Twain_

THE CHAINS of habit are often too small to be felt . . . until they are too strong to be broken. — _Anonymous_

IT has often been said, "What you are will determine what you do." Not always. You may be much better than your worst act, and you may be much worse than your best act. What you habitually do is you. — _Alfred A. Montapert_

HAPPINESS

HAPPINESS is the meaning and the purpose of life, the whole aim and end of human existence. — _Aristotle_

THE most blessed kind of happiness is a state of basic contentment. St. Paul said, "In whatever state I find myself, I have learned to be content." — _Alfred A. Montapert_

IT is the happiness that comes from within that is lasting and fulfilling. — _Leddy Schmelig_

WE are never so happy or so unhappy as we suppose.
— _La Rochefoucauld_

HAPPINESS

I ACCEPT life unconditionally. Life holds so much . . . so much to be happy about always. Most people ask for happiness on condition. Happiness can be felt only if you don't set any conditions.

— *Arthur Rubinstein*

HAPPINESS is in the taste, and not in the things themselves; we are happy from possessing what we like, not from possessing what others like.

— *La Rochefoucauld*

REMEMBER that happiness is as contagious as gloom. It should be the first duty of those who are happy to let others know of their gladness.

— *Maurice Maeterlinck*

NEVER forget that those who bring happiness to the lives of others cannot keep it from themselves.

— *Maurice Maeterlinck*

THE time to be happy is now; the place to be happy is here.

— *Robert G. Ingersoll*

REMEMBER this . . . that very little is needed to make a happy life.

— *Marcus Aurelius*

THE greatest obstacle to happiness is to expect too much happiness.

— *Bernard Le Bovier De Fontenelle*

HAPPINESS is something to accompany our living, striving, and pursuing, not to follow it. We must look for happiness along the road . . . not at the end of it. Cheerfulness must be made a constant daily habit. There is a tremendous amount of satisfaction to be gotten out of the hardest journeys through life.

— *Alfred A. Montapert*

THAT man is never happy for the present is so true that all his relief from unhappiness is only forgetting himself for a little while. Life is a progress from want to want, not from enjoyment to enjoyment.

— *Dr. Samuel Johnson*

THE greatest happiness in life is the conviction that we are loved, loved for ourselves ... say, rather, loved in spite of ourselves.
— *Victor Hugo*

IF we are to experience happiness, then what we think must be happy.
— *Ernest Holmes*

A HAPPY life is one which is in accordance with its own nature.
— *Seneca*

THE happiest and most contented people are those who each day perform to the best of their ability.
— *Alfred A. Montapert*

HAPPINESS sneaks in through a door you didn't know you left open.
— *John Barrymore*

HAPPINESS consists in the attainment of our desires, and in having only right desires.
— *St. Augustine*

HAPPINESS is the most important product of our life.
— *Alfred A. Montapert*

THE habit of being happy enables one to be freed, or largely freed, from the domination of outward conditions.
— *Robert Louis Stevenson*

THE Eternal Quest of Mankind Depends Upon ... THE CHARACTER OF YOUR THOUGHTS ... SOME VOCATION WHICH SATISFIES THE SOUL ... THE ABILITY TO GIVE VALUE TO YOUR EXISTENCE. For happiness depends upon what lies between the soles of your feet and the crown of your head.
— *Alfred A. Montapert*
The Way To Happiness

EAT with the Rich, but go to play with the Poor, who are capable of Joy.
— *Logan Pearsall Smith*

GET your happiness out of your work or you will never know what happiness is.
— *Elbert Hubbard*

HARVEST

LIFE is a gift, committed to OUR care. Keep everything in your life in line with the WORD OF GOD, and you will reap a HARVEST.

— *Alfred A. Montapert*

HEALING

GOD heals, and the doctor takes the fee.   — *Benjamin Franklin*

DIET cures more than doctors.   — *Old Adage*

GOD'S WORD is GOD'S MEDICINE. God heals by HIS WORD. FAITH comes by hearing, and hearing by the WORD OF GOD. According to your FAITH be it done unto you! — *Alfred A. Montapert*

EXERCISE is the Key to Healing. Exercise impels oxygen to flow into the blood stream which takes it through the body to all the organs. Exercise tones the muscles. Oxygen is LIFE!

— *Dr. Gus Hoehn*

THERE is no healing possible apart from God's Laws, whether they be natural (as we know them) or supernatural (as we have yet to learn them). That is a "heavy lesson."   — *Alfred A. Montapert*

HEALTH

GOOD health should be natural. Such innate resistance gives the individual a strength, a boldness, which he does not possess when his survival depends on physicians.   — *Alexis Carrel*

IT is interesting, and at times astounding, to consider how people, the most intelligent of all animals, are more prone than any other creature to indulge in excesses and practices they well know to be detrimental to their health.   — *H. Lamont Pugh, M.D.*

USE your health, even to the point of wearing it out. That is what it is for. Spend all you have before you die; and do not outlive yourself.
— *George Bernard Shaw*

YOU possess a natural ability to bring health to your body.
— *Evelyn M. Monahan*

NEGATIVE thinking is depriving people of their natural birthright of health. It is the prime cause in shortening the lives of so many of us. And yet it is so simple to live a healthier, longer . . . and so much happier . . . life. We have only to recognize how God works His wonders through laws governing nature and "human nature."
— *Walter M. Germain*

THE best of all medicines are resting and fasting. — *Benjamin Franklin*

YOUR health is your most important asset.   — *Alfred A. Montapert*

IF a rich man wishes to be healthy, he must live like a poor one.
— *Sir Richard Temple*

THE doctor of the future will give no medicine but will interest his patients in the care of the human frame, in diet, and in the cause and prevention of disease.   — *Thomas Alva Edison*

TECHNIQUES TO LIVE LONGER:
1. Avoid smoking, heavy drinking and overeating.

2. Keep physically active, exercise.

3. Eat simple nutritious foods, moderation in all things.

4. Avoid stress, or learn how to cope with it.

5. Have a belief in God and observe the Golden Rule.

6. Have a good sense of humor, laugh a lot.

7. Have a strong will to live and remain personally independent.
— *Alfred A. Montapert*

HEALTH

FEASTINGS are the physician's harvest.   — *Anonymous*

I'VE never met a healthy person who worried much about his health, or a good person who worried much about his soul.
                                                        — *John B. S. Haldane*

A SOUND BODY . . . a good mind . . . an honest purpose, and a lack of fear . . . are the essential elements of success. — *Alfred A. Montapert*

HEALTH is a precious thing . . . the only thing indeed that deserves to be pursued at the expense not only of time, sweat, labor, worldly good, but of life itself; since without health life becomes a burden and an affliction. Without health, pleasures, wisdom, knowledge lose their color and fade away. To my mind, no way that leads to health can be rugged, no means dearly bought.   — *Michel de Montaigne*

SCIENCE today confirms what religion has intuitively known from time immemorial, that faith, love and hope can work miracles of healing and restoration.   — *Joseph H. Krimsky*

HEALTH is certainly more valuable than money, because it is by health that money is procured.   — *Samuel Johnson*

LOOK to your health and if you have it, praise God, and value it next to a good conscience; for health is the second blessing that we mortals are capable of; a blessing that money cannot buy.
                                                        — *Sir Isaak Walton*

ONE hundred hears ago, when life expectancy was a great deal shorter, the major causes of illness and death were infectious diseases. NOW we are made ill by stress, which we attempt to minimize in a variety of unhealthy ways . . . alcohol, drugs, tobacco, gambling, spending sprees, overeating.   — *Alfred A. Montapert*

HEART

AS a man thinketh IN HIS HEART, so is he.

— Proverbs 23:7

THE HEART is wiser than the intellect.   *— Josiah G. Holland*

FOR where the heart is, that is sure to be where your treasure is.

— Anonymous

TWO things are hard on the heart: running upstairs and running down people.   *— Bernard Baruch*

A MERRY heart doeth good like a medicine . . . But a broken spirit drieth the bones.   *— Proverbs 17:22*

BETTER a heart full of love than a mind filled with knowledge.

— Charles Dickens

HEAVEN

TO get to heaven we must take it with us.   *— Henry Drummond*

NO man will go to heaven unless he first creates it within himself.

— Alfred A. Montapert

HELL

THE road to hell is paved with good intentions.

— Karl Marx

IF you don't believe there is a hell, just read the daily newspaper and you will soon find out.   *— Alfred A. Montapert*

HELP/HELPING

WHEN you row another person across the river, you get there yourself.
— *Anonymous*

HE helps others most, who shows them how to help themselves.
— *A.P. Gouthey*

THOSE who invest themselves in helping others, are involved in the most important work on the face of the earth. They are helping to complete God's plan.
— *Eric Hoffer*

IT is not your DUTY to help another out of his troubles, but it is your privilege, and if exercised, it may bring you priceless benefits.
— *Alfred A. Montapert*

HERO

NO MAN is a hero to his valet. This is not because the hero is no hero, but because the valet is a valet.
— *Georg Wilhelm F. Hegel*

HISTORY

HISTORY is the biography of great men.
— *Thomas Carlyle*

HISTORY is not history unless it is the truth.
— *Abraham Lincoln*

HISTORY repeats itself. That's one of the things wrong with history.
— *Clarence Darrow*

WE learn from history that we do not learn from history.
— *Georg Wilhelm F. Hegel*

MAN is explicable by nothing less than all his history.
— *Ralph Waldo Emerson*

HOME

HOME is the place where, when you have to go there, they have to take you in.
— *Robert Frost*

HE is happiest, be he king or peasant, who finds his peace in home.
— *Goethe*

TO be happy at home is the ultimate result of all ambition; the end to which every enterprise and labor tends, and of which every desire prompts the prosecution.
— *Samuel Johnson*

HOME is a place not only of strong affections, but of entire unreserve; it is life's undress rehearsal, its back room, its dressing-room, from which we go forth to more careful and guarded intercourse, leaving behind us much debris of cast-off and everyday clothing.
— *Harriet B. Stowe*

HONESTY

I HOPE that I shall always possess firmness and virtue enough to maintain what I consider the most enviable of all titles, the character of an "Honest Man."
— *George Washington*

WHEN in doubt, tell the truth.
— *Mark Twain*

IT is never too late to tread the path of honesty.
— *Seneca*

WHATEVER games are played with us, we must play no games with ourselves, but deal in our privacy with the last honesty and truth.
— *Ralph Waldo Emerson*

HONESTY

MEN are seldom more innocently employed than when they are honestly making money. — *Samuel Johnson*

HOPE

THERE is no medicine like HOPE, no incentive so great, and no tonic so powerful, as an expectation of something tomorrow. It is HOPE that maintains most of mankind. — *Alfred A. Montapert*

I STEER my bark with hope in the head, leaving fear astern. — *Thomas Jefferson*

GOD created the world for reasons that are sufficient unto Himself. It is not necessary that we be told these reasons. As long as we know that God loves us, we have a base for hope. And when we have hope, all else can be born with patience. — *Edward J. Carnell*

HOPE ever urges on and tells us tomorrow will be better. — *Tibullus*

HUMAN NATURE/HUMANITY

THE perversity of human nature is the greatest of the mysteries of human life. — *Arnold J. Toynbee*

THE deepest need in human nature is the craving to be appreciated! — *William James*

JUST as true humor is laughter at oneself, true humanity is knowledge of oneself. — *Alan Watts*

TRUE human progress is based less on the inventive mind than on the conscience. — *Albert Einstein*

I DO not have a very high opinion of the bulk of mankind. I feel that the irrational forces in man's nature are so strong that the rational forces have little chance of success against them. A small minority may be able to live a life of reason, but most men are more comfortable living with their delusions and superstitions than with the truth.
— *Sigmund Freud*

THE history of the world is the record of man in quest of his daily bread and butter.
— *Henrik Van Loon*

HUMILITY

HUMILITY, the first test of a truly great man.
— *John Ruskin*

DON'T be so humble, you're not that great.
— *Golda Meir*

IF you would grow great and stately, you must try to walk sedately.
— *Robert Louis Stevenson*

IF the best man's faults were written on his forehead, he would draw his hat over his eyes.
— *Anonymous*

HUMOR

HUMOR is medicine for many a trouble, and a dose of laughter is good for most of our ills. It relieves nervous tension and acts as a shock absorber for the bumps of life.
— *Alfred A. Montapert*

THERE is nothing more serious in man than his sense of humor. It is the sign that he wants all the truth and sees more sides of it than can be soberly and systematically stated.
— *Mark Van Doren*

IDEA

NEARLY every man who develops an idea works it up to the point where it looks impossible, and then he gets discouraged. That's not the place to become discouraged. — *Thomas Alva Edison*

MAN'S mind, once stretched by a new idea, never regains its original dimensions. — *Oliver Wendell Holmes*

ALL achievement, all earned riches, have their beginning in an idea! — *Napoleon Hill*

WHETHER the ideas that come your way are great or small, it is what you do with them that shapes your life.

— *A.H.Z. Carr*

IDEALS

IDEALS are like stars; you will not succeed in touching them with your hands. But like the seafaring man on the desert of waters, you choose them as your guides, and following them you will reach your destiny. — *Charles Schurz*

MANKIND has a greater need of the IDEAL than of the REAL. It is by the real that we exist; it is by the IDEAL that we live. The love of God is man's highest ideal. The difference is, some men merely exist, while others truly live. — *Alfred A. Montapert*

WHEN the world seems large and complex, we need to remember that great world ideals all began in some home neighborhood.

— *Konrad Adenauer*

OUR ideals are the blueprints of our lives. — *Roy L. Smith*

WE become what we love. If we love what is base, we become base; but if we love what is noble, we become noble. Hence the importance of the right kind of ideals and the right kind of heroes. Our Lord said, "Where your treasure is, there is your heart also.

— *Fulton J. Sheen*

IF

THE word "IF" is often highly significant. Think how different it would have been:
If you had only kept silent.
If you had listened to good advice.
If you had been more patient.
If you had frankly apologized.
If you had acted with prudence.
If you had shunned that bad investment.
If you had shown more sympathy.
If you had taken daily exercise.
If you had avoided that accident.
If you had started early.
If you had not run into debt.
If you had always been on time.
If you had promptly declined.
If you had controlled your temper.
If you had put it into writing.
If you had said the right word.
If you had eaten in moderation.
If you had stayed at home.
If you had not blundered.
If you had been industrious
If you had guarded your health.
If you had recognized your fault.
If you had simply agreed.
If you had daily prayed.
If you had persevered.
If you had given more generously.
If you had not been stubborn.

— *Alfred A. Montapert*

IGNORANCE

NOTHING is more terrible to see than ignorance in action. — *Goethe*

IGNORANCE is weakness. — *Plato*

EVERYBODY is ignorant, only on different subjects.
— *Will Rogers*

THE recipe for perpetual ignorance is: Be satisfied with your opinions and content with your knowledge. — *Elbert Hubbard*

IT is difficult to get a man to understand something when his salary depends upon his not understanding it. — *Upton Sinclair*

WHEN I was a boy of fourteen, my father was so ignorant I could hardly stand to have the old man around. But when I got to be twenty-one, I was astonished at how much he had learned in seven years. — *Mark Twain*

HE who knows little quickly tells it. — *Italian Proverb*

IMAGINATION

WHAT is now proved was once only imagined. — *William Blake*

HOLD a Success Picture of yourself in your mind's eye of what you would like to Be ... Do ... Have. Successful living starts with your SUCCESS PICTURE. — *Alfred A. Montapert*

IMAGINATION grows by exercise. — *W. Somerset Maugham*

SOME men see things as they are and say, "Why?" I dream things that never were and say, "Why not?" — *Henry David Thoreau*

IMAGINATION

IT is well to remember that there is no patent or restrictions of any kind on imagination. Flights of fancy can take you anywhere you want to go. You can live in an unreal DREAM WORLD or you can harness the unlimited resources of imagination so that you can have anything and everything you want. — *Howard E. Hill*

IMAGINATION rules the world. — *Napoleon Bonaparte*

WHATEVER one man is capable of conceiving, other men will be able to achieve. — *Jules Verne*

ALL religion, all art, all finance, all business, every ship at sea, every bridge that spans the gulf, and every discovery in the great world of science owes its origin, its inception, its first impulse to the exercise of that strange gift, imagination . . . a power to make images. — *S. Parkes Cadman*

IMAGINATION is making new holes out of familiar parts. — *H. A. Overstreet*

IMAGINATION is as good as many voyages . . . and much cheaper. — *Alfred A. Montapert*

GREAT living starts with a picture, held in your imagination, of what you would like to do or be. — *Harry E. Fosdick*

IMITATION

IT is by imitation, far more than by precedent, that we learn everything; and what we learn thus, we acquire not only more effectually, but more pleasantly. Thus forms our manners, our opinions, our lives. — *Edmund Burke*

IMITATION

WE are more than half of what we are by imitation. The great point is to choose good models and to study them with care.

— *Lord Chesterfield*

IMITATION is born with us, but what we ought to imitate is not easily found.

— *Goethe*

EXCEPT to an ignoramus or intellectualist, nothing imitative can equal that which is imitated. Instead of imitating effects, search for the principle that made them original, and own your own effects.

— *Frank Lloyd Wright*

IMMORTALITY

I HAVE never understood why people worry about exactly what form immortality takes. We have to accept what is in store for us, so why worry about it? The incentive for us to live to the best of our ability every minute of our lives lies in this fact of immortality.

— *Eleanor Roosevelt*

SURELY God would not have created such a being as man, with an ability to grasp the infinite, to exist only for a day! No, man was made for immortality.

— *Abraham Lincoln*

REMEMBER that what you possess in the world, will be found at the day of your death to belong to someone else, but what you are, will be yours forever.

— *Henry Van Dyke*

IMPATIENCE

THERE is a limit at which forbearance ceases to be a virtue.

— *Edmund Burke*

WHICH of you by taking thought can add one cubit unto his stature?

— *Matthew 6:27*

IMPORTANT

WHAT is important is that we should produce something of value to society.
— *Jawaharlal Nehru*

THINK and do things in order of their importance.
— *Henry Doherty*

KEEP your life simple. Decide what is important and what is unimportant and do not waste yourself on unimportant issues. Save your thoughts and energies and put both to use on the things that count.
— *Rhoda Lachar*

IMPOSSIBLE

TO get PROFIT without RISK, EXPERIENCE without DANGER, and REWARD without WORK, is as impossible as it is to LIVE without being BORN.
— *Alfred A. Montapert*

WE are interested in doing the impossible. What else is worth doing?
— *Dr. Christopher Hills*

FEW things are impossible to diligence and skill.
— *Samuel Johnson*

EVERY noble work is at first impossible.
— *Thomas Carlyle*

NOTHING is impossible; there are ways which lead to everything; and if we had sufficient will we should always have sufficient means.
— *La Rochefoucauld*

IN my vocabulary there is no such word as "can't" because I recognize that my abilities are given to me by God to do what needs to be done.
— *Wofford B. Camp*

IMPULSE

HE that takes time to think and consider will act more wisely than he that acts hastily and on impulse.   — *Charles Simmons*

CALCULATION is of the head, impulse is of the heart; and both are good in their way.   — *Henry Giles*

A TRUE history of human events would show that a far larger proportion of our arts are the result of sudden impulses and accident, than of that reason of which we so much boast.   — *William Cowper*

ACT upon your impulses, but pray that they may be directed by God.   — *E. Tennent*

INCENTIVE

WE are so conditioned by our competitive society that we are almost incapable of action without the incentive of personal profit, personal prestige and personal power.   — *Alfred A. Montapert*

INCENTIVE: What a little word, but oh! what big things it can do. It furnishes the strongest driving force known to man. It creates a real interest in doing things. If we could discover a formula to arouse in all of us a real interest in doing the right sort of things, we would revolutionize the world.   — *William Ross*

TO those who clamor for more "incentive" I would reply, "What greater incentive can there be than to preserve our freedoms without which all material possessions are worthless?"   — *Bernard Baruch*

INCENTIVES are spurs that goad a man to do what he doesn't particularly like, to get something he does particularly want.
                                                — *Paul G. Hoffman*

INDECISION

INDECISION is a great waster of power.
— *O. S. Marden*

THE best way out is through.
— *Robert Frost*

THERE is no more miserable human being than the one in whom nothing is habitual but indecision.
— *William James*

INDEPENDENCE

I DO not choose to be a common man. It is my right to be uncommon ... if I can. I seek opportunity, not security. I do not wish to be a kept citizen, humbled and dulled by having the company look after me. I want to take the calculated risk, to dream and to build, to fail and to succeed. I refuse to barter incentive for a dole. I prefer the challenges of life to the guarantee existence, the thrill of fulfillment to the stale calm of utopia. I will not trade freedom for beneficence, nor dignity for a handout. It is my heritage to think and act for myself, enjoy the benefit of my creations, and to face the world boldly and say, This I have done.
— *Herbert C. Hoover*

WHAT is it that makes so many of us easy targets for silver-tongued orators and their catchwords? First, it's easier to accept slogans than to think things through for ourselves. Second, it's safer to string along with the crowd than to stand alone. Many of the greatest men of history were ridiculed while they lived. That was because they stood alone. They dared to defy ancient customs. They refused to string along.
— *William Benton*

HAVE the courage to be independent if you can, and act independently if you may.
— *Leszczynski Stanislaw I*

INDIVIDUAL/INDIVIDUALITY

WHOSO would be a man must be a non-conformist.

— *Ralph Waldo Emerson*

INDIVIDUALITY is the salt of life. You may have to live in a crowd but you do not have to live like it, nor subsist on its food.

— *Henry Van Dyke*

WHENEVER you find that you are on the side of the majority, it is time to reform. — *Mark Twain*

EACH individual is the center of a world that exists only for him. He is unique, specific, and possesses qualities that are found only in himself. Each human being is a unique event in space and time. This event . . . it is ourselves. — *Alexis Carrel*

EVERY great institution is the lengthened shadow of a single man.

— *Ralph Waldo Emerson*

IF a man does not keep pace with his companions perhaps it is because he hears a different drummer. Let him step to the music he hears however measured and far away. — *Henry David Thoreau*

THE strongest man in the world is he who stands most alone.

— *Henrik Ibsen*

NOT nations, not armies, have advanced the race; but here and there, in the course of ages, an individual has stood up and cast his shadow over the world. — *E. H. Chapin*

GOD gave every man individuality of constitution, and a chance for achieving individuality of character. He puts special instruments into every man's hands by which to make himself and achieve his mission.

— *J. G. Holland*

INDUSTRY

WHEN I hear a young man spoken of as giving promise of high genius, the first question I ask about him is always, "Does he work?"
— *John Ruskin*

A MAN who gives his children habits of industry provides for them better than giving them a fortune.   — *Bishop Richard Whately*

INFLUENCE

YOUR mother, father, teacher, clergyman, friend have built their influences into your character.   — *Wilfred Peterson*

MANY a man has owed his influence far more to character than to ability.   — *John Lubbock*

INFLUENCE is exerted by every being from the hour of birth to that of death.   — *E. H. Chapin*

INHERIT/INHERITANCE

FEW realize that, in order to retain an inherited fortune, one must assume great responsibilities and worries, while, at the same time, the greatest source of happiness and contentment . . . the joy of working and striving to attain . . . has been taken away. — *William Ross*

GOD'S "Providence" is my Inheritance.   — *Alfred A. Montapert*

WHAT madness is it for a man to starve himself to enrich his heir, and so turn a friend into an enemy: For his joy at your death will be proportionate to what you leave him.   — *Seneca*

THE meek shall inherit the earth . . . but not the oil rights.
— *J. Paul Getty*

INHERIT/INHERITANCE

OUR inheritance of well founded, slowly conceived codes of honor, morals and manners, the passionate convictions which so many hundreds of millions share together of the principles of freedom and justice, are far more precious to us than anything which scientific discoveries could bestow.
— *Winston Churchill*

INITIATIVE

INITIATIVE is doing the right thing without being told.
— *Victor Hugo*

THERE is no more valuable subordinate than the man to whom you can give a piece of work and then forget it, in the confident expectation that the next time it is brought to your attention that it will be done in the form of a report that the thing has been done.
— *Clifford Pinchot*

INNER LIFE

THE great within is always greater than the great without.
— *Alfred A. Montapert*

WHAT lies behind us and lies before us are small matters compared to what lies within us.
— *Ralph Waldo Emerson*

THE inner world gives meaning to the outer world.
— *Woellner*

THE foundation of a person's REAL SECURITY is his Inner Strength: Attitude, Beliefs, Courage, High Ideals, Standards and Character, Faith in himself and God, Love and Discipline. These traits give Encouragement, Inner Joy and Goodness.
— *Alfred A. Montapert*

INSPIRATION

SOME men have thousands of reasons why they cannot do what they want to, when all they need is one reason why they can.
— *Dr. Willis R. Whitney*

NO man was ever great without some divine inspiration. — *Cicero*

INSPIRATION, the manner in which one single ray of light, one single precious hint, will clarify and energize the whole mental life of him who receives it, is among the most wonderful and heavenly of intellectual phenomena. — *Arnold Bennett*

A TEACHER who is attempting to teach without inspiring the pupil with a desire to learn, is hammering on cold iron. — *Horace Mann*

GENIUS is one percent inspiration and ninety-nine percent perspiration. — *Thomas Alva Edison*

WHAT is the inspiration of the writer, or the discovery of the scientist? It is the constructive creation of his intuitive consciousness at work. — *Walter M. Germain*

WE should get into the habit of reading INSPIRATIONAL BOOKS, looking at INSPIRATIONAL PICTURES, hearing INSPIRATIONAL MUSIC, associating with INSPIRATIONAL FRIENDS.
— *Alfred A. Montapert*

WE all need someone who inspires us to do better than we know how. — *Anonymous*

INTEGRITY

NOTHING is at last sacred but the integrity of our own mind.
— *Ralph Waldo Emerson*

INTELLECT/INTELLIGENCE

THERE are one-story intellects, two-story intellects, and three-story intellects with skylights. All fact collectors who have no aim beyond their facts are one-story men. Two-story men compare, reason, generalize, using the labor of the fact collectors as their own. Three-story men idealize, imagine, predict; their best illumination comes from above, through the skylight.

— Oliver Wendell Holmes

THE difference between intelligence and education is this ... that intelligence will make you a good living.   *— Charles Kettering*

INTUITION

ALL great discoveries are made by men whose feelings run ahead of their thinkings.   *— C. H. Parkhurst*

THE intellect has little to do on the road to discovery. There comes a leap in consciousness, call it intuition or what you will, and the solution comes to you, and you know not how or why. All great discoveries are made in this way.   *— Albert Einstein*

INTUITION is given only to him who has undergone long preparation for receiving it.   *— Louis Pasteur*

INTUITION resembles ... the seemingly instinctive impulse of the scientist toward a discovery, the creative inspiration of the artist, or the immediate appraisals made by great executives or great judges.

— Alexis Carrel

INTUITION is a guess that made good.   *— Robert Hardwicke*

INVESTMENT

THE only good investment is to invest with God in things that will be at par when all things else have no value at all.

— *Alfred A. Montapert*

INVESTIGATE before you invest, no matter if the salesman is in a hurry to catch the noon train. — *Roy L. Smith*

AN investment in knowledge pays the best interest.

— *Benjamin Franklin*

ONE of the things I learned as a farm boy was, you save the best seed for planting so you will have a good harvest . . . the best corn . . . the best potatoes . . . the best seed for lettuce, beets, cabbage, and cauliflower. The same with money . . . you NEVER spend your "SEED MONEY." You INVEST YOUR SEED MONEY. You spend the money you make off the money you invest, so you are ALWAYS RICH. — *Alfred A. Montapert*

JEALOUSY

JEALOUSY is the art of injuring ourselves more than others.

— *Alexandre Dumas*

JOY

JOY is not in things, it is in us. — *Charles Wagner*

HAPPY is the person who not only sings, but feels God's eye is on the sparrow, and knows He watches over me. To be simply ensconsed in God is true Joy. — *Alfred A. Montapert*

JOY

THERE is no joy in life like the joy of sharing. — *Billy Graham*

JOY in one's work is the consummate tool. — *Phillips Brooks*

JOY is a deep spiritual union with the unchanging God. A man's life, said Jesus Christ, is not fulfilled, nor is it filled full of, nor by, the abundance of things which he possesses. Here is one of the most important statements ever given to a bewildered, heart-hungry world. Joy, then, is a living spring hidden deep in the inner life that is no more dependent upon things than the sunrise is dependent upon a cock's crowing. — *A. P. Gouthey*

JUDGES

FOUR things belong to a judge: to hear courteously, to answer wisely, to consider soberly, and to decide impartially. — *Socrates*

A JUDGE who cannot punish associates himself in the end with the criminal. — *Goethe*

JUDGES ought to be more learned than witty, more reverent than plausible, and more advised than confident; above all things, integrity is their portion and proper virtue. — *Sir Francis Bacon*

IT is the judge's business to answer to the question of law, the jury's to answer to the question of fact. — *Latin Proverb*

JUDGMENT

I MISTRUST the judgment of every man in a case in which his own wishes are concerned.

— *Arthur Wellesley*
Duke of Wellington

JUDGMENT

JUDGE a man by his questions rather than by his answers.

— Voltaire

JUDGMENT is not the knowledge of fundamental laws; it is knowing how to apply them. This necessitates experience. *— Charles Gow*

JUDGE not, that ye be not judged. *— Matthew 7:1*

THE senses do not deceive, but the judgment does. *— Goethe*

ALWAYS keep in mind the part that mood can play in affecting one's judgment of a piece of work; be cautious of enthusiasm when the sun shines bright, and slow to dismissal when the clouds hang low.

— J. Donald Adams

DAY OF JUDGMENT

THEN each shall be tried, and his works; not each one and his wealth, not each one and his office, not each one and his dignity, not each one and his power, but each one and his works.

— Chrysostom

JUSTICE

JUSTICE is the insurance which we have on our lives and property; and obedience is the premium which we pay for it. *— William Penn*

NEITHER the evening nor the morning star is more beautiful than justice. *— Aristotle*

JUSTICE is the bread of the nation; it is always hungry for it.

— Chateaubriand

JUSTICE

ALL justice comes from God . . . He is the sole source.   — *Rousseau*

THE aim of justice is to give everyone his due.   — *Cicero*

IT'S a good thing most of us do not get what's coming to us.
— *A.P. Gouthey*

JUSTICE without force is powerless; force without justice is tyranni-cal.   — *Blaise Pascal*

KINDNESS

KINDNESS is the oil that takes the friction out of life.
— *J.L. Newland*

LEAD the life that will make you kindly and friendly to everyone about you, and you will be surprised what a happy life you will lead.
— *Charles Schwab*

THERE is nothing so kingly as kindness.   — *Alice Cary*

I SHALL pass through this world but once. If, therefore, there be any kindness I can show, or any good thing I can do, let me do it now; let me not defer it or neglect it, for I shall not pass this way again.   — *Stephen Grellet*

HOW often a careless, unkind word spoken can spoil your day, wreck some big job or deal, hurt a loved one, lose a friend. Many of us, through ignorance, thoughtlessness, or want of judgment, wound those whom we love best and most wish to help.
— *Alfred A. Montapert*

BE ye kind to one another.   — *Ephesians 4:32*

KINDNESS is in our power, but fondness is not. — *Samuel Johnson*

TENDERNESS and KINDNESS are not signs of weakness and despair, but manifestations of strength and resolution. — *Kahlil Gibran*

WHO masters his passions and turns them to deeds of kindness is greater than a king. — *Lao Tzu*

KINGDOM OF GOD

"SEEK ye first the Kingdom of God and His righteousness, and all these other things will be added unto you." That constitutes the entire ministry of Jesus Christ. — *Alfred A. Montapert*

THE Kingdom of God is within you. — *Luke 17:21*

WHEN I think about the Kingdom of God, I am struck dumb by its grandeur; for the Kingdom of God is God Himself with all His fullness. — *Meister Eckhart*

KNOW/KNOWLEDGE

IT is knowing what to do with things that counts. — *Robert Frost*

YOU generally hear that what a man doesn't know doesn't hurt him, but in business what a man doesn't know does hurt. — *Elmo Lewis*

THE important thing for you is not how much you know ... but the quality of what you know. — *Erasmus*

WHAT do you know for sure? Actually all you know for sure is what you have experienced; the rest is speculation. — *Alfred A. Montapert*

KNOW/KNOWLEDGE

ONLY so much do I know, as I have lived. — *Ralph Waldo Emerson*

ALL men desire to know. — *Aristotle*

I AM not young enough to know everything. — *James M. Barrie*

IT is better to know some of the questions than all of the answers.
— *James C. Thurber*

HE who truly knows has no occasion to shout. — *Leonardo da Vinci*

KNOW thyself... wisdom is no more than the carrying out of this command. — *Michel de Montaigne*

KNOWLEDGE is the antidote of fear. — *William Brady*

WE do not need more knowledge, we need more character!
— *Calvin Coolidge*

KNOWLEDGE advances by steps, and not by leaps.
— *Thomas B. Macaulay*

WHAT is the use of knowledge if it serves no useful purpose?
— *Proverb*

WE live and grow by new knowledge. — *Thomas Alva Edison*

A COLLEGE education does not make an educated man. Lee Du Bridge, former president of Cal Tech, says, "The scientific man outside of his field is as dumb as the next guy." THE TRUE TEACHER IS LIFE ITSELF, and the world is the only schoolroom in which we can learn what we so evidently require.
— *Alfred A. Montapert*

KNOWLEDGE is nothing unless it is distilled into wisdom.
— *Roger Babson*

KNOW/KNOWLEDGE

KNOWLEDGE is of two kinds: We know a subject ourselves, or we know where we can find information upon it. — *Samuel Johnson*

OF all kinds of knowledge that we can ever obtain, the knowledge of God and the knowledge of ourselves are the most important.
— *Jonathan Edwards*

LABOR

HONEST labor bears a lovely face. — *T. Dekker*

LABOR is preferable to idleness, as brightness to rust. — *Plato*

LABOR, if it were not necessary for the existence, would be indispensable for the happiness of man. — *Samuel Johnson*

IF you want knowledge, you must toil for it; if food, you must toil for it; and if pleasure you must toil for it; toil is the law.
— *John Ruskin*

LABOR is life. — *Thomas Carlyle*

LABOR is God's education. — *Ralph Waldo Emerson*

LANGUAGE

LANGUAGE is a very imperfect instrument of expression.
— *John Lubbock*

THE LANGUAGE denotes the man; a coarse or refined character finds its expression naturally in a coarse or refined phraseology.
— *Christian N. Bovee*

LAUGHTER

THE most wasted of all days is that on which one has not laughed.
— *Nicolas Chamfort*

LAUGH and live long . . . Laughter is a TONIC.
— *Alfred A. Montapert*

LAW/LAWS

THERE is but one law for all; namely, that which governs all law, the law of our Creator, the law of humanity, justice, equity; the law of nature and of nations. — *Edmund Burke*

THERE is tangible evidence to be seen everywhere that there is intelligence and purposefulness in all that exists, from atom to man to galaxy, functioning according to law. — *Willis Kinnear*

A LAW may be defined as a rule laid down for the guidance of an intelligent being, by an intelligent being having power over him.
— *Austin*

COMMON LAW is man-made law and is that which each community lays down and applies to its own members. UNIVERSAL LAW is the law of NATURE, which comes from the Highest Power . . . GOD.
— *Alfred A. Montapert*

MAN-MADE laws are man's way of dividing things. — *Unknown*

WHEN the state is most corrupt, then laws are most multiplied.
— *Tacitus*

OPINIONS alter, manners change, creeds rise and fall, but the moral laws are written on the table of eternity. — *Lord Acton*

GOD'S LAW

THE QUALITY of every person's life is determined by the knowledge of and use of THE LAWS OF GOD which are built into the very structure of man's nature. To discover and obey these laws is the highest of human enterprises. — *Alfred A. Montapert*

THE Ten Commandments are not laws. They are THE LAW.
— *Cecil B. DeMille*

ALL our knowledge of things is derived from God, in and by the order of nature. — *Ethan Allen*

LAWS OF LIFE

THE rules of life are found within yourself. Ask yourself constantly, "What is the right thing to do?" — *Confucius*

HAVE a dream and believe in it. Strong dreams always come true. My greatest passion is to spell out the LAWS OF LIFE. To understand nature's laws and mysteries that hold everything together.
— *Alfred A. Montapert*

OBEDIENCE to the laws of life prevents the excesses of individualism which incessantly set man against man. — *Alexis Carrel*

NATURAL LAWS

THE knowledge of the natural laws, and the power given us by this knowledge over the material world, and also over human beings, alone are of importance. — *Alexis Carrel*

NATURE'S LAWS affirm instead of prohibiting. If you violate her laws, you are your own prosecuting attorney, judge, jury and hangman. — *Luther Burbank*

NATURE'S Laws are the invisible government of the earth.
— *Alfred A. Montapert*

NATURAL LAWS

WHEN the laws of human nature are thoroughly understood they are nature's guide. They reveal the specific way to proceed in any given situation. They help you know how to determine which choices to make.   — *Alfred A. Montapert*

WE NEED to review and obey the NATURAL LAWS OF MAN'S NATURE, for they are the only sound starting point to the right and basic way to every man's betterment. When we obey the natural laws we are rewarded with health, with happiness and success. This is Nature's reward to induce us to obey her laws. When we violate the universal laws the result is pain, disease, discontent, lack of harmony and material failure.   — *Alfred A. Montapert*

NATURAL laws . . . are universal and inexorable. In no country can they be disobeyed without penalty. Nor do they ever warn the transgressor; the punishment is as silent as the command. — *Unknown*

EVERY Person Has FREE CHOICE . . . Free to Obey or Disobey the NATURAL LAWS. YOUR CHOICE Determines the Consequences.   — *Alfred A. Montapert*

THERE is a sense of solidity about the NATURAL LAWS which belongs to nothing else in the world. Here, at last, amid all that is shifting, is one thing sure; one thing outside ourselves, unbiased, unprejudiced, uninfluenced by like or dislike, by doubt or fear; one thing that holds its way to be eternally incorruptible and undefiled. In these Laws one stands face to face with truth, solid and unchangeable.   — *Henry Drummond*

EVERYONE in the Universe . . . as well as the Universe itself, including the Constellations, Nature, and every Beast and Fowl, and every form of life including Man . . . is governed by Nature's Laws. Man lives in Law as fish live in water. This is the secret of the wise.   — *Alfred A. Montapert*

LAWYERS

DISCOURAGE litigation. Persuade your neighbor to compromise whenever you can. As a peacemaker the lawyer has a superior opportunity of being a good man. There will still be business enough.
— *Abraham Lincoln*

THERE is no such thing as a friendly lawsuit.   — *Alfred A. Montapert*

A MAN who acts as his own lawyer has a fool for a client.
— *Anonymous*

LAZINESS

A YOUNG man idle, an old man needy.   — *Italian Proverb*

THE man who sits down in the pasture and waits for the cow to back up to him to be milked will go without milk.   — *A.P. Gouthey*

THE trouble with loafing is it leaves you without a loaf.
— *Alfred A. Montapert*

LEADER/LEADERSHIP

WHEN you are getting kicked from the rear, it means you're in front.   — *Fulton Sheen*

THE man who is worthy of being a leader of men will never complain of the stupidity of his helpers, of the ingratitude of mankind, nor of the inappreciation of the public. These things are all part of the great game of life, and to meet them and not go down before them in discouragement and defeat, is the final proof of power.   — *Elbert Hubbard*

A LEADER is a dealer in hope.   — *Napoleon Bonaparte*

LEADER/LEADERSHIP

THE best leaders are those most interested in surrounding themselves with assistants and associates smarter than they are ... being
frank in admitting this ... and willing to pay for such talents.

— *Amos Parrish*

IT is possible to give commands in such a manner as to inspire an
intense desire to obey. — *Maj. Gen. J.M. Schofield*

THE good general makes good soldiers. — *Latin Proverb*

FOR every man who has the ability to lead, there are a thousand
men waiting to be led. — *Roy L. Smith*

LEARN/LEARNING

LEARN, but learn from the learned. — *Cato*

GIVE thyself time to learn something new and good, and cease to be
whirled around. — *Marcus Aurelius*

WHAT is college? An institution of learning. What is a business? An
institute of learning. Life itself is an institute of learning.

— *Thomas Alva Edison*

LEARNING, if rightly applied, makes a young man thinking, atten-
tive, industrious, confident, and wary; and an old man cheerful and
useful. It is an ornament in prosperity, a refuge in adversity, the
entertainment at all times; it cheers in solitude, and gives moderation
and wisdom in all circumstances. — *Ray Palmer*

A LEARNED man has always wealth in himself. — *Phaedrus*

YOU cannot teach a man anything; you can only help him to find it
for himself. — *Galileo*

LEARN/LEARNING

STUDY and in general the pursuit of truth and beauty is a sphere of activity in which we are permitted to remain children all our lives.
— *Albert Einstein*

IF your EDUCATION consists only in what you got from books, it will not be complete until you've had a postgraduate course in Experience. — *Alfred A. Montapert*

KNOWLEDGE must be gained by ourselves. Mankind may supply us with facts; but the results, even if they agree with previous ones, must be the work of our mind. — *Benjamin Disraeli*

LEARNING is finding out what you already know. Doing is demonstrating that you know it. — *Richard Bach*

LIFE is a great continuing and inspiring adventure . . . You learn until your last breath. — *Alfred A. Montapert*

THE true lover of learning then must from his earliest youth, as far as in him lies, desire the truth. — *Plato*

PUPILS must not be encouraged to think that there are shortcuts to knowledge. — *Bertrand Russell*

I AM still learning. — *Michelangelo*

IF I shall not be learning now, when shall I be? — *Lacydes of Cyrene*

LEARNING is a treasure which follows its owner everywhere.
— *Chinese Proverb*

IT is man's privilege to live always learning, but never knowing.
— *Anonymous*

LEISURE

TEMPTATION rarely comes in working hours. It is in their leisure time men are made or marred.
— *W.M. Taylor*

HE enjoys true leisure who has time to improve his soul's estate.
— *Henry David Thoreau*

LETTERS

IN a man's letters his soul lies naked; his letters are only the mirror of his breast.
— *Samuel Johnson*

TO correspond with those I love is among my highest gratifications.
— *George Washington*

LIAR

NO man has a good enough memory to make a successful liar.
— *Abraham Lincoln*

LIBERAL

I CAN remember way back when a liberal was one who was generous with his own money.
— *Will Rogers*

LIBERTY

LIBERTY is not the power of doing what we like, but the right of being able to do what we ought.
— *Lord Acton*

FREE people, remember this maxim: We may acquire liberty, but it is never recovered if it is once lost.
— *Jean Jacques Rousseau*

LIBERTY will not descend to a people; a people must raise themselves to liberty; it is a blessing that must be earned before it can be enjoyed. — *Charles Caleb Colton*

WE of this generation should never forget that men first came to America, not to find soil for their ploughs, but to secure liberty for their souls . . . Freedom to worship God. — *Unknown*

LIBRARY

MY library shelves are the corridors of time. All the world is around me, all that ever stirred human hearts or fired the imagination is harmlessly here. — *Alfred A. Montapert*

NEVER lend books, for no one ever returns them; the only books I have in my library are books that other folks have lent me.
— *Anatole France*

A GREAT library contains the diary of the human race. The great consulting room of a wise man is a library. — *G. Dawson*

LIFE

TO improve the golden moment of opportunity, and catch the good that is within our reach, is the great art of life. — *Samuel Johnson*

LIFE is a battle for what is right. No man lives without jostling and being jostled; in all ways he has to elbow himself through the world, giving and receiving offense. LIFE is a battle . . . it is a fight from start to finish . . . a struggle for survival from womb to grave.
— *A.P. Gouthey*

YOUTH is a blunder; manhood is a struggle; old age a regret.
— *Benjamin Disraeli*

LIFE

THE Bible says: "This is life, and life eternal, that you may know God." To know is to experience, to have fellowship, to enjoy, to appreciate. Life is measured by the number of things you are alive to. Life is effectiveness, life is power, correspondence to environment. I must take the Power of God and have inside fellowship with Him. Use this Power for my personal development. GOD IS NOT ONLY SPIRIT, BUT LIFE ITSELF. — *Alfred A. Montapert*

LIFE would be infinitely happier if we could only be born at the age of eighty and gradually approach eighteen. — *Mark Twain*

LIFE is like the sea, never at rest, untamed . . . perilous! The secret of its everlasting interest lies precisely here, that you cannot explain it, and never know what is going to happen next! — *W. Dixon*

LIFE is not dated merely by years. Events are sometimes the best calendars. — *Benjamin Disraeli*

THOUGH we seem grieved at the shortness of life in general, we are wishing every period of it at an end. The minor longs to be of age, then to be a man of business; then to make up an estate, then to arrive at honors, then to retire. — *Joseph Addison*

ANYONE can carry his burden, however heavy, until nightfall. Anyone can do his work, however hard, for one day. Anyone can live sweetly, patiently, lovingly, purely, till the sun goes down. And this is all that life ever really means. — *F.R.L. Newbery*

ENJOY LIFE NOW! It will never be better. — *Alfred A. Montapert*

A WELL-ORDERED life is like climbing a tower; the view halfway up is better than the view from the base, and it steadily becomes finer as the horizon expands. — *William L. Phelps*

LIFE

LIFE is to be enjoyed . . . to laugh, to sing, to love, to meditate.
— *Alfred A. Montapert*

TO SEE life as struggle rather than reward, mental rather than environmental, spiritual rather than material, eternal rather than temporal, is to move into a new mind and is to live as a real person is meant to live. — *John H. Miller*

LIFE is no brief candle to me. It is a sort of splendid torch which I have got hold of for the moment, and I want to make it burn as brightly as possible before handing it on to future generations.
— *George Bernard Shaw*

OUR lives are like a candle in the wind. — *Carl Sandburg*

WE must make up for the threatened brevity of life by heightening the intensity of it. — *Joshua L. Liebman*

THE complete life, the perfect pattern, includes old age as well as youth and maturity. The beauty of the morning and the radiance of noon are good, but it would be a very silly person who drew the curtains and turned on the light in order to shut out the tranquility of evening. — *W. Somerset Maugham*

THE fool, with all his other faults, has this also: he is always getting ready to live. — *Epicurus*

YOU get out of LIFE what you put into it. You reap the harvest from the seeds YOU PLANT. It's all up to you. — *Alfred A. Montapert*

LET us LIVE, while we are alive! — *Goethe*

REMEMBER that life is neither pain nor pleasure; it is serious business, to be entered upon with courage and in a spirit of self-sacrifice. — *Alexis de Tocqueville*

LIFE

LIFE is a progress, and not a station. — *Ralph Waldo Emerson*

THE truth taught by Jesus Christ is the right way to live. What He taught is not primarily a revelation. He is God's revelation of how life must be lived to be lived at its best. — *A.P. Gouthey*

THERE is no cure for birth or death save to enjoy the interval.
— *George Santayana*

LIFE is a succession of Lessons, which must be lived to be understood. — *Ralph Waldo Emerson*

THE great object in living is to attain more life ... more in QUALITY as well as QUANTITY. — *Julian S. Huxley*

ONE of the most tragic things I know about human nature is that all of us tend to put off living. We are all dreaming of some magical rose garden over the horizon ... instead of enjoying the roses that are blooming outside our windows today. — *Dale Carnegie*

IT is a funny thing about life; if you refuse to accept anything but the best, you very often get it. — *W. Somerset Maugham*

THE cost of a thing is the amount of what I call LIFE which is required to be exchanged for it, immediately or in the long run.
— *Henry David Thoreau*

I DO not know what I may appear to the world; but to myself I seem to have been only a boy playing on the seashore, and diverting myself in now and then finding a smoother pebble or a prettier shell than ordinary, while the great ocean of truth lay all undiscovered before me. — *Sir Isaac Newton*

LIFE can only be UNDERSTOOD ... backward; but it must be LIVED ... forward. — *Soren Kierkegaard*

I LOOK back on my life like a good day's work, it was done and I feel satisfied with it. I was happy and contented, I knew nothing better and made the best out of what life offered. And life is what we make it, always has been, always will be. — *Grandma Moses*

ETERNAL LIFE

"I AM come that you may have life," Jesus said. Not a philosophy about life, not a set of do's and don'ts: "I am come that they might have life." This is His entire Gospel in epitome. Everything He did and said centers here. — *Alfred A. Montapert*

HE that findeth his life shall lose it; and he that loseth his life for my sake shall find it. — *Matthew 10:39*

AND this is Life Eternal, that they might know Thee, the only true God, and Jesus Christ, whom Thou hast sent. — *John 17:3*

NATURE never makes haste; her systems revolve at an even pace. The buds swell imperceptibly, without hurry or confusion, as though the short spring days were an eternity. Why, then, should man hasten as if anything less than eternity were allotted for the least deed? — *Henry David Thoreau*

VERILY, verily, I say unto you, He that believeth on me hath everlasting life. — *John 6:47*

BELIEF in Christ guarantees everlasting life to the believer. And why? Because Christ is the life principle. In Him there is no death, only life, vibrant and continuous. When we become identified with Him through faith, the life principle which is in Him develops also in us. The more we become like Him through spiritual growth, we share His eternity. — *Norman Vincent Peale*

ETERNAL LIFE

THE great use of a life is to spend it for something that outlasts it.
— *William James*

THE sole purpose of life in time is to gain merit for life in eternity.
— *St. Augustine*

THE truest end of life is to know that life never ends. — *William Penn*

THE GOOD LIFE/QUALITY OF LIFE

THE quality of life is more important than life itself.   — *Alexis Carrel*

THE good life is one inspired by love and guided by knowledge.
— *Bertrand Russell*

LIFE AT ITS BEST should be a harmonious adjustment of NECES-
SITY and DESIRE, of what MUST BE DONE, and WHAT WE
SHOULD LIKE TO DO. MODERATION and SIMPLICITY are two
of the most important words in the dictionary and the wise man
incorporates them into his life. Going at an even pace, rather than
spurts, makes the best use of energy and intellect. In the rush of life
we have forgotten in part how to live. We have forgotten how to find
simple things charming. The adventure of taking a walk, joy in the
sunlight, birds and flowers, is not for poets only, but for everyone
who has eyes to see and ears to hear.   — *Alfred A. Montapert*

THE best things are nearest: Breath in your nostrils, light in your
eyes, flowers at your feet, duties at your hand, the path of right just
before you. Then do not grasp at the stars, but do life's plain,
common work as it comes, certain that daily duties and daily bread
are the sweetest things in life.   — *Robert Louis Stevenson*

THE good life is not only good for one's conscience; it is good for art,
good for knowledge, good for health, good for fellowship.
— *Lewis Mumford*

THE GOOD LIFE/QUALITY OF LIFE

DO not worry; eat three square meals a day; say your prayers; be courteous to your creditors; keep your digestion good; exercise; go slow and easy. Maybe there are other things that your special case requires to make you happy, but, my friend, these I reckon will give you a good life. — *Abraham Lincoln*

SELL yourself on NOW as the Best Years of Your Life and on your own powers to enjoy them. Take time to smell the flowers. Say with Monte Cristo, "The world is mine." Relax and have all the fun you want while you can still enjoy the sea, the flowers, the song of a bird, and the laughter of children. Learn to truthfully say, "I have never been happier in my life than now." This is the wisdom of the well-lived life. — *Alfred A. Montapert*

AND he said to them, Take heed, and beware of covetousness: for a man's life consisteth not in the abundance of the things which he possesseth. — *Luke 12:15*

I STILL find each day too short for all the thoughts I want to think, all the walks I want to take, all the books I want to read, and all the friends I want to see. The longer I live the more my mind dwells upon the beauty and the wonder of the world. One's own door opens upon the wealth of heaven and earth. Life is a struggle, but not a warfare; is but a day's labor on God's earth, under the sun and stars, with other laborers, where we may think and sing and rejoice as we work. — *John Burroughs*

THAT man lives twice who lives the first life well. — *Robert Herrick*

THE key to the abundant life is the revelation of God to human hearts. — *Alfred A. Montapert*

DO ANY human beings ever realize life while they have it? Every, every minute? — *Thornton Wilder*

WAY OF LIFE

"YOU cannot serve God and Mammon." Neither can you walk forward and backward at the same time. Only fools try it.

— *Alfred A. Montapert*

TO LIVE a long time and be productive is everyone's dream. It all depends upon your way of life.　　　　— *Alfred A. Montapert*

MY theory is to enjoy life, but the practice is against it.

— *Charles Lamb*

LIKE

EACH man is led by his own liking.　　　　　　　— *Virgil*

I LIKE strawberry ice cream, but when I go fishing I use worms . . . 'cause the fish like worms.　　　　　　　　— *Unknown*

LIMITATIONS

HE who has no inclination to learn more will be very apt to think that he knows enough.　　　　　　　— *Thomas Powell*

AS LONG as a man stands in his own way, everything seems to be in his way.　　　　　　　　— *Henry David Thoreau*

NOT doing more than the average is what keeps the average down.

— *William Winans*

WHEN a man has put a limit on what he will do, he has put a limit on what he can do.　　　　　　　— *Charles Schwab*

IT is a profound error to presume that everything has been discovered; it is to take the horizon which bounds the eye for the limit of the world.　　　　　　　　— *A.M. Lemierre*

YOU all have powers you never dreamed of. You can do things you never thought you could do. There are no limitations in what you can do except the limitations in your own mind as to what you cannot do. Don't think you cannot. Think you can.   — *Darwin Kingsley*

WE must learn our limits; we are all something, but none of us are everything.   — *Blaise Pascal*

LISTEN

I LIKE to listen. I have learned a great deal from listening carefully. Most people never listen.   — *Ernest Hemingway*

KNOW how to listen, and you will profit even from those who talk badly.   — *Plutarch*

HEAR the other side.   — *St. Augustine*

LITTLE THINGS

IT has long been an axiom of mine that the little things are infinitely the most important.   — *Arthur Conan Doyle*

MEN trip not on mountains, they trip on molehills.   — *Chinese Proverb*

LIVE/LIVING

WHEN men speak ill of you, live so as nobody may believe them.   — *Plato*

EACH thing lives according to its kind; the heart by love, the intellect by truth, the higher nature of man by intimate communion with God.   — *E.H. Chapin*

LIVE/LIVING

BE not afraid because some time thou must cease to live, but fear never to have begun truly to live. — *Marcus Aurelius*

LIVE your life so that whenever you lose, you are ahead.
— *Will Rogers*

TO know God is to live. — *Leo Tolstoy*

THE most important thing to learn in life ... is how to live. More men have ruined themselves than have ever been destroyed by others. No one has ever been able to show that any change in the laws of Nature would be for the better. We bring the troubles of life on ourselves, by our own errors ... errors in both senses, by doing what we know all the time to be wrong, but also, and perhaps almost as much, by our mistakes. — *Alfred A. Montapert*

FAR better it is to dare mighty things, to win glorious triumphs, even though checkered by failure ... than to take rank with those poor spirits who neither enjoy much nor suffer much, because they live in the gray twilight that knows not VICTORY nor DEFEAT.
— *Theodore Roosevelt*

WE never live; we are always in the expectation of living.
— *Francois Voltaire*

LIFE is for living ... and living well. — *Alfred A. Montapert*

LIFE belongs to the living, and he who lives must be prepared for changes. — *Goethe*

HOW vain it is to sit down to write when you have not stood up to live! — *Henry David Thoreau*

THE first duty of life is to live ... to live as completely as possible ... to increase life for oneself and for others, to make it more elevated, more sweet, and more beautiful. — *Alexis Carrel*

HE who has a WHY to live can bear with any HOW.

— *Friedrich Nietzsche*

WE say of almost any crisis hour, "These are the times that try men's souls." Well, my observation is that just ordinary everyday living is the severest test of all. The fellow who keeps steadily on his way when there is no unusual stress of circumstances to force the issue is a hero indeed. — *Alfred A. Montapert*

LONGEVITY

TO KNOW how to grow old is the master work of wisdom, and one of the most difficult chapters in the great art of living. — *Henri Amiel*

THERE is no shortcut to longevity. To win it is the work of a lifetime. — *Sir James Browne*

THERE are no guarantees for you of a long life . . . but your chances of living a long while seem BEST if you come from a long-lived family, EXERCISE MORE and EAT LESS. — *Dr. Henry G. Bieler*

LOOKING AHEAD

PREPARE yourself well for the years ahead. Picture your entire life from now to the end. Plan the fulfillment of your major objective . . . Peace . . . Happiness . . . Contentment throughout your existence!

— *Alfred A. Montapert*

LOOKING BACK

IT'S but little good you'll do, watering last year's crops. Yet that is exactly what I have seen hundreds of my patients doing in the past twenty-five years . . . watering with freely flowing tears things of the irrevocable past. — *Dr. Frederic Loomis*

LOSS

A MAN who loses his money, gains, at the least, experience, and sometimes, something better. — *Benjamin Disraeli*

HE who loses wealth loses much; he who loses a friend, loses more; but he that loses his courage loses all. — *Miguel de Cervantes*

WISE men never sit and wail their loss, but cheerly seek how to redress their harms. — *William Shakespeare*

LOVE

LOVE is the Great Transformer . . . LOVE transforms:
 Ambition into aspiration,
 Greed into gratitude,
 Selfishness into service,
 Getting into giving,
 Demands into dedication,
 Loneliness into happiness. — *Unknown*

PAINS of love be sweeter far
Than all other pleasures are. — *John Dryden*

LOVE is the fulfilling of life's law. — *Elbert G. Hubbard*

LIKE the sun, love radiates and warms into life all that it touches. — *O.S. Marden*

LOVE is the light and sunshine of life. We are so constituted that we cannot fully enjoy ourselves, or anything else, unless someone we love enjoys it with us. Even if we are alone, we store up our enjoyment in hope of sharing it hereafter with those we love. — *John Lubbock*

LOVE

THE course of true love never did run smooth. — *William Shakespeare*

WE love the things we love for what they are. — *Robert Frost*

THE measure of one's devotion is doing, not merely saying. Love is demonstration, not merely declaration. — *Anonymous*

LOVE is the normal state of being, the state that puts you into entire harmony with all the laws of God and Nature, gives wings to your thoughts, inspiration to your efforts, and success to your enterprises. — *Louis M. Grafe*

HOW do I love thee? Let me count the ways . . . — *Elizabeth Barrett Browning*

NO scientific discovery was so fraught with significance as the revelation of the law of love by Jesus the Crucified. For this law is, in fact, that of the survival of human societies. — *Alexis Carrel*

LOVE essentially is good will: Thinking well of others and wishing them well. It is a state of the will, not of the animal passions. Even in its earthiest form it is a giving as well as a taking. People who cannot give themselves never can know love. — *Mortimer J. Adler*

IT was Dante's deathless love for Beatrice that gave rise to his sublimest thinking. — *Alfred A. Montapert*

EYE hath not seen nor ear heard, neither have entered into the heart of men, the things which God has prepared for them that love Him. — *1 Corinthians 2:9*

TO free oneself of love a person need only concentrate on his own problems. — *Latin Proverb*

LOVE

EACH one has a mission to fulfill, a mission of love. At the hour of death when we come face to face with God, we are going to be judged on love; not on how much we have done, but how much love we have put into our actions.   *— Mother Teresa of Calcutta*

LOVE alone shall discover the heart of God at the heart of man; love alone shall reveal the Self to the self, and find enthroned in the high citadel of the secret place of God in our own heart that beneficence which embraces the whole world.   *— Ernest Holmes*

LOVE is the highest Principle that Life has to give us because it is Life acting in unity with itself.   *— Ernest Holmes*

WE are shaped and fashioned by what we love.   *— Goethe*

THE tragedy of love isn't death or separation, the tragedy of love is indifference.   *— W. Somerset Maugham*

LOVE gives naught but itself and takes naught but from itself. Love possesses not nor would it be possessed; for love is sufficient unto love.   *— Kahlil Gibran*

HOW hard is the life of him who asks for love and receives passion!
                    — Kahlil Gibran

ONCE you have learned to love, you have learned to live.
                    — Walter M. Germain

To love and win is the best thing. To love and lose, the next best.
                    — William M. Thackeray

THE story of love is not important. What is important is that one is capable of love. It is perhaps the only glimpse we are permitted of eternity.   *— Helen Hayes*

LOVE is ever the beginning of Knowledge, as fire is of light.
— *Thomas Carlyle*

SOME DAY, after man has tried everything else, we shall wake up and develop the LOVE which Jesus Christ brought into the world. The LOVE which would act as a cement to bind all men together in brotherly love.
— *Alfred A. Montapert*

LOYALTY

LOYALTY is the noblest word in the catalogue of social virtue.
— *John Ruskin*

LOYALTY is one thing that a leader cannot do without.
— *Alfred A. Montapert*

LOYALTY is what we seek in friendship.
— *Cicero*

THE one, absolute, unselfish friend that man can have in this selfish world, the one that never deserts him, the one that never proves ungrateful or treacherous, is his dog.
— *Senator Vest*

LUCK

SHALLOW men believe in luck. Strong men believe in cause and effect.
— *Ralph Waldo Emerson*

I AM a great believer in luck. The harder I work the more of it I seem to have.
— *Coleman Cox*

TO a brave man, good and bad luck are like the right and left hand. He uses both.
— *St. Catherine*

FOOLS do not know how clearly linked are luck and merit. — *Goethe*

LUXURY

MOST of the luxuries, and many of the so-called comforts of life, are not only dispensable, but positive hindrances to the elevation of mankind.
— *Henry David Thoreau*

MACHINE

ONE machine can do the work of fifty ordinary men. No machine can do the work of one extraordinary man.
— *Elbert G. Hubbard*

MAN

IN man, the things which are not measurable are more important than those which are measurable.
— *Alexis Carrel*

EVERY man is a fluid that becomes solid, a treasure that grows poorer, a history in the making, a personality that is being created.
— *Alexis Carrel*

MAN, regardless of his cleverness, his achievements and his gadgets, is a spiritual pauper without God.
— *Billy Graham*

WHAT man is before God, that he is and no more.
— *St. Francis of Assisi*

MAN'S inhumanity to man . . . makes countless thousands mourn.
— *Robert Burns*

THE evolution of man is slow. The injustice of man is great.
— *Oscar Wilde*

MAN is BODY . . . MIND . . . SPIRIT. Each part affects the other. Each part must be developed. We must take the whole man and not part of him.
— *Alfred A. Montapert*

MAN

WHOEVER considers the study of anatomy, I believe, will never be an athiest; the frame of man's body and the coherence of his parts, being so strange and paradoxical, that I hold it to be the greatest miracle of nature.   — *Edward Herbert*

A MAN'S ability cannot possibly be of one sort and his soul of another. If his soul is well-ordered, serious and restrained, his ability also is sound and sober. Conversely, when the one degenerates, the other is contaminated.   — *Seneca*

WE are all sculptors and painters, and our material is our own flesh and blood and bones.   — *Henry David Thoreau*

EVERY man is tasked to make his life, even in its details, worthy of the contemplation of his most elevated and critical hour.
— *Henry David Thoreau*

A MAN is the facade of a temple wherein all wisdom and all good abide.   — *Ralph Waldo Emerson*

ALL things work exactly according to their quality, and according to their quantity; attempt nothing they cannot do, except man only.
— *Ralph Waldo Emerson*

MAN is the miracle of miracles, the great, inscrutable mystery of God.   — *Alexis Carrel*

THE more I see of man . . . the more I like dogs.   — *Madam de Stael*

MAN is more evil because his reasoning ability permits him to devise evil pursuits. He may appear to be animal when functioning on his lowest level. But an animal cannot devise evil. Man is a separate and distinct being from every other creature on earth, and probably heaven.   — *A.P. Gouthey*

MANKIND

THE proper study of mankind is man. — *Alexander Pope*

MAN is a spiritual being, housed in a body. We have all the equipment to enable us to maintain contact with God and reality. St. Augustine says, "We are built for God and unhappy we will be if we do not maintain this fellowship." — *Alfred A. Montapert*

IN order to love mankind, expect but little from them; in order to view their faults without bitterness we must accustom ourselves to pardon them, and to perceive that indulgence is a justice which frail humanity has a right to demand from wisdom.
— *Edward Bulwer-Lytton*

MANNERS

GOOD manners is the art of making those people easy with whom we converse; whoever makes the fewest people uneasy, is the best bred man in the company. — *Jonathan Swift*

GOOD manners are made up of petty sacrifices.
— *Ralph Waldo Emerson*

MARRIAGE

A GOOD wife maketh a good husband. — *John Heywood*

THE young man who wants to marry happily should pick out a good mother and marry one of her daughters . . . any one will do.
— *J. Ogden Armour*

AS a general rule, people marry most happily with their own kind. The trouble lies in the fact that people usually marry at an age where they do not really know what their own kind is. — *Robertson Davies*

MAN scans with scrupulous care the character and pedigree of his horses, cattle, and dogs before he matches them; but when he comes to his own marriage he rarely, or never, takes any such care.

— *Charles R. Darwin*

MASTERPIECE

WHEN love and skill work together, expect a masterpiece.

— *John Ruskin*

MATERIALISM

THE world has to learn that the actual pleasure derived from material things is of rather low quality on the whole and less even in quantity than it looks to those who have not tried it.

— *Oliver Wendell Holmes*

MATURITY

THE later years of life should properly be its crowning glory . . . Growth in stature and physical strength may cease at twenty-five, but head and heart, intellect, soul and spirit keep on growing throughout the span of life. The later years of life, in personal satisfactions to be gained as well as in opportunities for service to humanity, must be regarded as the richer years of life.   — *Alfred A. Montapert*

WHAT is maturity? It is being able to carry money without spending it; being able to bear an injustice without retaliation; being able to do one's duty even when one is not watched; being able to keep on the job until it is finished; being able to accept criticism without letting it whip you.   — *Anonymous*

ONLY the years ripen . . . A person does not reach maturity until he has fifty years of EXPERIENCE and OBSERVATION. The world is full of green apples, that's why it has the bellyache.

— *Alfred A. Montapert*

MAXIMS

MAXIMS of 85-year-old M. Gabriel Honataux: Anything can happen . . . Everything is forgotten . . . Every difficulty can be overcome . . . No one understands anything . . . If everyone knew what everyone said about everyone, no one would speak to anyone . . . Above all things, never be afraid . . . The enemy who forces you to retreat is himself afraid of you at that very moment. — *Andre Maurois*

MEDITATION

MEDITATION is the life of the soul; action, the soul of meditation; honor, the reward of action. — *Francis Quarles*

THE art of meditation is letting God speak to me. We should be silent that we might hear the whisper of God. — *Alfred A. Montapert*

MEMORY

IT is certain that the memory is the only receptacle, not only of philosophy, but of all that concerns the conduct of life, and of all the arts. — *Cicero*

MEMORY is the scribe of the soul. — *Oscar Wilde*

THE true art of memory is the art of attention. — *Samuel Johnson*

MEMORY, we are told, is the gallery in which the master artist of the years gone by hangs his rarest pictures. — *Alfred A. Montapert*

WHEN time, who steals our years away,
Shall steal our pleasures too,
The memory of the past will stay,
And half our joys renew.

— *Thomas Moore*

MENTAL HEALTH

OF the thousands of mentally and emotionally abnormal I have observed over a number of years, I believe that the one most frequent denominator among them has been lack of worthy purpose in life.
— *James T. Fisher*

MERCY

AMONG the attributes of God, although they are all equal, mercy shines with even more brilliancy than justice.   — *Miguel de Cervantes*

THE quality of mercy is not strained,
It droppeth as the gentle rain from heaven
Upon the place beneath. It is twice blest;
It blesses him that gives and him that takes.   — *William Shakespeare*

MERIT

REAL merit of any kind cannot long be concealed; it will be discovered, and nothing can depreciate it but a man exhibiting it himself. It may not always be rewarded as it ought; but it will always be known.
— *Lord Chesterfield*

WE must not judge of a man's merits by his qualities, but by the use he makes of them.
— *La Rochefoucauld*

CHARMS strike the sight, but merit wins the soul. — *Alexander Pope*

CONTEMPORARIES appreciate the man rather than his merit; posterity will regard the merit rather than the man.
— *Charles Caleb Colton*

TRUE merit is like a river, the deeper it is the less noise it makes.
— *Lord Halifax*

MERRY

A MERRY heart doeth good like a medicine, but a broken spirit drieth the bones. — *Proverbs 17:22*

MERRY have we met, and merry have we been; Merry let us part, and merry meet again. — *Old English Adage*

MAN is the merriest, the most joyous of all the species of creation. Above him and below him all are serious. — *Joseph Addison*

METHOD

THERE is always a best way of doing everything, even if it be to boil an egg. — *Ralph Waldo Emerson*

BE methodical if you would succeed in business, or in anything. Have a work for every moment, and mind the moment's work. — *William Mathews*

METHOD goes far to prevent trouble in business; for it makes the task easy, hinders confusion, saves abundance of time, and instructs those who have business pending, what to do and what to hope. — *William Penn*

GOD works through men. Men are his method. That's the way He gets things done. That's the way He has designed the system. — *Frederick K. C. Price*

MIND

IN order to improve the mind, we ought less to learn, than to contemplate. — *Rene Descartes*

THE MIND is the door to the Heart. Your Heart the arena of FAITH. "Trust in the Lord with all thine Heart, and lean not to thine own understanding." — *Proverbs 3:5*

YOUR Mind can make or break you! It takes in, digests and gives meaning to your every experience. It initiates and regulates your every thought, emotion, action . . . conscious or unconscious.
— *Alfred A. Montapert*

THE human mind will not be confined to any limits. — *Goethe*

THE mind ought sometimes to be diverted, that it may return the better to thinking. — *Phaedrus*

EVERY human mind feels pleasure in doing good to another.
— *Thomas Jefferson*

IF your mind and its affections be pure, and sincere, and moderate, nothing shall have the power to enslave you. — *Thomas a Kempis*

A SIMPLE and independent mind does not toil at the bidding of any prince. — *Henry David Thoreau*

GREAT minds have purposes, others have wishes. Little minds are tamed and subdued by misfortune; but great minds rise above them.
— *Washington Irving*

THE immature mind hops from one thing to another; the mature mind seeks to follow through. — *Harry A. Overstreet*

THE mind is its own place, and in itself
Can make a Heav'n of Hell, a Hell of Heav'n. — *John Milton*

OF the universal mind each individual man is one more incarnation. All its properties consist in him. — *Ralph Waldo Emerson*

IF a man be endowed with a generous mind, this is the best kind of nobility. — *Plato*

KEEP your mind open, but remember, it's not a sieve.
— *Alfred A. Montapert*

MIND

'TIS the mind that makes the body rich. — *William Shakespeare*

THE only thing about a man that is a man . . . is his MIND. Everything else you can find in a pig or a horse. — *Archibald Macleish*

THERE will always be a frontier where there is an open mind and a willing hand. — *Charles F. Kettering*

IT is the mind that makes the man, and our vigor is in our immortal soul. — *Ovid*

MIRACLES

WHO believes in miracles nowadays? I DO! I have seen too many to be mistaken. Miracles just as remarkable as the resurrection of Lazarus, after being four days dead. Just as remarkable as converting water into wine, as Jesus did. The days of miracles are only past for the person who does not believe. — *Unknown*

MISERS

MISERS mistake gold for their good; whereas it is only a means of attaining it. — *La Rochefoucauld*

WHEN I caution you against being a miser, I do not therefore advise you to become a prodigal or a spendthrift. — *Horace*

A MERE madness, to live like a wretch, and die rich. — *Robert Burton*

MISFORTUNE

THE greatest misfortune of all is not to be able to bear misfortune. — *Bias*

MISHAPS are like knives, that either serve us or cut us, as we grasp them by the blade or the handle. — *J.R. Lowell*

COURAGE has more resources against misfortune than has reason.
— *Vauvenargues*

THINK of the ills from which you are exempt. — *Joseph Joubert*

MISTAKES

TO make mistakes is human, but to profit from them is divine.
— *Elbert G. Hubbard*

LIFE, like war, is a series of mistakes; and he is not the best Christian nor the best general who makes the fewest false steps. Poor mediocrity may secure that; but he is the best who wins the most splendid victories by the retrieval of mistakes. — *F.W. Robertson*

NO man ever became great or good except through many and great mistakes. — *William Gladstone*

WE learn wisdom from failure much more than from success; we often discover what will do, by finding out what will not do; and probably he who never made a mistake never made a discovery.
— *Samuel Smiles*

MODERATION

EVERYTHING in excess is opposed to nature. — *Hippocrates*

EVERYTHING that exceeds the bounds of MODERATION has an unstable foundation. — *Seneca*

ONLY actions give life strength; only moderation gives it charm.
— *Jean Paul Richter*

MODERATION

MODERATION is one of the most important words in the dictionary and in life.   — *Alfred A. Montapert*

OUT of moderation a pure happiness springs.   — *Goethe*

MOMENT

HE who seizes the moment is the right man.   — *Goethe*

MOST of us never learn that it is as impossible to recapture a lost moment as it is to recapture the sunshine of yesterday.

— *A.P. Gouthey*

MONEY

MONEY often costs too much.   — *Ralph Waldo Emerson*

IF money be not your servant, it will be your master. The covetous man cannot so properly be said to possess wealth, as that it may be said to possess him.   — *Francis Bacon*

MONEY is not required to buy one necessity of the soul.

— *Henry David Thoreau*

MEN seldom profit by money except that which they earn.

— *Andrew Carnegie*

VIRTUE has never been as respectable as money.   — *Mark Twain*

I DON'T like money, actually, but it quiets my nerves.   — *Joe Louis*

THE love of money is the root of all evil.   — *1 Timothy 6:10*

MONEY is neither right nor wrong per se. It only becomes right or wrong when the HEART of us is involved with it.
— *Alfred A. Montapert*

THE happiest time in any man's life is when he is in red-hot pursuit of a dollar with a reasonable prospect of overtaking it. — *Josh Billings*

IT'S an old and much ridiculed bromide that money can't buy happiness, but there's a great deal of truth to these words.
— *J. Paul Getty*

HAPPINESS lies not in the mere possession of money; it lies in the enjoyment of achievement, in the thrill of creative effort.
— *Franklin D. Roosevelt*

MONEY MANAGEMENT

LIVE within your income. Always have something saved at the end of the year. Let your imports be more than your exports, and you'll never go far wrong. — *Samuel Johnson*

MANAGING money usually requires more skill than making it.
— *Roy L. Smith*

THE most common money mistake is not having a financial plan . . . a comprehensive strategy to deal with inflation, taxes, family protection, retirement and the other challenges you face, both today and tomorrow. Most people are so busy making money that they devote little attention to managing it. — *Alfred A. Montapert*

MORALITY

SOCIAL righteousness may be expressed in laws, but it lives only in the moral vigilance of the people. — *Borden P. Bowne*

MORALITY

KNOWLEDGE and skills alone cannot lead humanity to a happy and dignified life. Humanity has every reason to place the proclaimers of high moral standards and values above the discoverers of objective truth. — *Albert Einstein*

LAW can elevate society, but it cannot reach the principles from which our behavior springs. Back of constitutions, back of laws, back of administrations, there must be a moral code which is the power and glory of all human governments. — *Billy Graham*

MORALITY is of more importance to us than any or all other attainments. — *Ethan Allen*

THE definition of good and evil is based both on reason and on the immemorial experience of humanity. — *Alexis Carrel*

WHEN a man acts according to the law of his nature, he cannot be sinning. — *Bhagavad-Gita*

MOTHER

A MAN never sees all that his mother has been to him, until it is too late to let her know that he sees it. — *W. D. Howells*

IN the heart of some of us is the memory of a GOOD MOTHER. A home of prayer where spiritual influence surrounded us like the air we breathe. Where at an old-fashioned family altar of prayer, we learned early in life the importance of these first things. That memory not only lingers with us, but is the dominant force and power in our lives to this day. — *Alfred A. Montapert*

ALL that I am, or hope to be, I owe to my angel Mother! — *Abraham Lincoln*

GIVE me the mothers of the nation to educate, and you may do what you like with the boys. — *Garibaldi*

MOTIVATION

MOVE out, Man! Life is fleeting by.
Do something worthwhile, before you die.
Leave behind a work sublime
That will outlive you, and time. — *Alfred A. Montapert*

DESPERATION is sometimes as powerful an inspirer as genius.
— *Benjamin Disraeli*

LET a man conceive an ambition, recognize a duty, espouse a cause, and how every organ in his body and every faculty of his mind begins to function smoothly and effectively as never before! — *Councillor*

I LIKE it when my men get excited, for that is when we get more business. — *Walter P. Chrysler*

MOTIVES

MOTIVES are invisible . . . but they are the true test of character.
— *Alfred A. Montapert*

A MAN generally has two reasons for doing a thing. One that sounds good, and a REAL one. — *J. Pierpont Morgan*

MUSIC

MUSIC is the voice of God . . . The grand object of music is to touch the heart. — *Alfred A. Montapert*

EVERY man, when at work, even alone, has a song, however rude, to soften his labor. — *Quintilian*

MUSIC is the only language in which you cannot say a mean or sarcastic thing. — *John Erskine*

NAME

A GOOD name is rather to be chosen than great riches, and loving favor rather than silver and gold. *— Solomon*

GOOD name, in man or woman, is the immediate jewel of their souls. Who steals my purse steals trash; but he that filches from me my good name, robs me of that which not enriches him, and makes me poor indeed. *— William Shakespeare*

I WOULD rather make my name than inherit it.
— William Makepeace Thackeray

NATURE

YOU may drive out Nature with a pitchfork, but she will ever hurry back, to triumph in stealth over your foolish contempt. *— Horace*

EARTH and sky, woods and fields, lakes and rivers, the mountain and the sea, are excellent schoolmasters, and teach some of us more than we can ever learn from books. *— John Lubbock*

ALL are but parts of one stupendous whole,
Whose body Nature is and God the soul. *— Alexander Pope*

HE that strives against NATURE will forever strive in VAIN.
— Samuel Johnson

NATURE is only to be commanded by obeying her.
— Sir Francis Bacon

TRUE it is that Nature speaks to those who have eyes to see and ears to hear. The world and all that is therein was made by God, and must of necessity be one unit. The Laws which control in the natural realm must control in the spiritual realm. *— Alfred A. Montapert*

NATURE

THE first in time and the first in importance of the influences upon the mind is that of nature. Every day, the sun; and after sunset, night and her stars. Ever the winds blow; ever the grass grows ... There is never a beginning, there is never an end, to the inexplicable continuity of this web of God, but always circular power returning into itself. Therein man resembles his own spirit, whose beginning, whose ending, he never can find ... so entire, so boundless.
— Ralph Waldo Emerson

NATURE cannot be surprised in undress. Beauty breaks in everywhere.
— Ralph Waldo Emerson

NATURE is the living, visible garment of God.
— Goethe

NATURE understands no jesting. She is always true, always serious, always severe. She is always right and the errors are always those of man. She despises the man incapable of appreciating her, and only to the apt, the pure and the true does she reveal her secrets.
— Goethe

NATURE will bear the closest inspection. She invites us to lay our eye level with her smallest leaf, and take an insect view of its plain.
— Henry David Thoreau

NATURE abhors a vacuum, and if I can only walk with sufficient carelessness I am sure to be filled.
— Henry David Thoreau

IT is only necessary to behold thus the least fact or phenomenon, however familiar, from a point a hair's breadth aside from our habitual path or routine, to be overcome, enchanted by its beauty and significance.
— Henry David Thoreau

INTO every empty corner, into all forgotten things and nooks, Nature struggles to pour life, pouring life into the death, life into life itself.
— Henry Beston

NECESSITY

IT is necessity and not pleasure that compels us.   *— Dante*

OUR necessities are few, but our wants are endless.   *— H.W. Shaw*

NEEDS

OUR chief want in life is somebody who shall make us do what we can.   *— Ralph Waldo Emerson*

IN the heart of every person there is a hunger, a longing for something that you cannot find in this world. It is the soul that longs for a comforting spirit, a fellowship with God, the Supreme Power.
    — Alfred A. Montapert

NEGATIVE

WE are all born into this world with germs of both positive and negative personality. As we mature, it is a simple matter of choice which one of these we wish to develop. If we choose to develop a positive pleasing personality, it is necessary to cultivate it just as you would cultivate the gardens and the fields to bring forth a good yield. If we choose the negative personality it requires no effort whatsoever, because it will grow, just as the weeds grow in the garden without any control, care or attention.   *— Dr. Paul Parker*

NEIGHBORS

LOVE your neighbor, yet pull not down your hedge.
    — George Herbert

NO one is rich enough to do without a neighbor.   *— Danish Proverb*

NEW

NOTHING is new but arrangement. — *Will Durant*

THEREFORE if any man be in Christ, he is a new creature: old things are passed away; behold, all things are become new.
— *II Corinthians 5:17*

NEWS

WHEN a dog bites a man, that is not news, because it happens so often. But if a man bites a dog, that is news. — *John B. Bogart*

NOW

YESTERDAY'S successes belong to yesterday with all yesterday's defeat and sorrows. The day is here. The time is now. — *Unknown*

PEOPLE spend their lives in anticipation of being extremely happy in the future. But all we own is the PRESENT . . . NOW. PAST opportunities are gone. FUTURE opportunities may or may not come. NOW is all we have . . . we must enjoy each day . . . one at a time. We are here on a short visit . . . be sure to smell the flowers.
— *Alfred A. Montapert*

OBEDIENCE

OBEDIENCE is the mother of success, the wife of safety.
— *Aeschylus*

THE man who has not learned to obey has trouble ahead of him every step of the way. The world has it in for him continually, because he has it in for the world. — *Elbert G. Hubbard*

OBEDIENCE

I SINCERELY wish people would put a little more emphasis upon OBEYING the LAW ... than they do complaining about my men and our struggle for its enforcement ... which is for everyone's benefit and preservation. — *Daryl Gates, Los Angeles Chief of Police*

OBSERVATION

YOU should not only have attention to everything, but a quickness of attention, so as to observe at once all the people in the room ... their motions, their looks and their words ... and yet without staring at them and seeming to be an observer. — *Lord Chesterfield*

OBSERVATION, not old age, brings wisdom. — *Publilius Syrus*

I AM a speculator. The word comes from the Latin *speculari*, which means "to observe". I observe. — *Bernard Baruch*

SEE everything ... OVERLOOK a great deal ... CORRECT a little. — *Pope John XXIII*

OBSTINACY

THERE is no mistake so great as that of always being right. — *Samuel Butler*

OPINION

ACCURATE knowledge is the basis of correct opinion; the want of it makes the opinions of most people of little value. — *Charles Simmons*

OPINION is ultimately determined by the feelings, and not by the intellect. — *Herbert Spencer*

PUBLIC opinion is everything. — *Will Rogers*

OPPORTUNITY

LOTS of people know a good thing the minute the other fellow sees it first. — *J.E. Hedges*

TO every man his chance, to every man, regardless of his birth, his shining golden opportunity. To every man the right to live, to work, to be himself, and to become whatever thing his manhood and his vision can contribute to make him. — *Thomas Wolfe*

YOU should hammer your iron when it is glowing hot. — *Publilius Syrus*

I WILL study and get ready, and perhaps my chance will come. — *Abraham Lincoln*

THERE is no security on this earth; there is only opportunity. — *Gen. Douglas MacArthur*

THE secret of success in life is for a man to be ready for his opportunity when it comes. — *Benjamin Disraeli*

NO great man ever complains of want of opportunity. — *Ralph Waldo Emerson*

A WISE man will make more opportunities than he finds. — *Sir Francis Bacon*

THERE is a tide in the affairs of men,
Which, taken at the flood, leads on to fortune;
Omitted, all the voyage of their life
Is bound in shallows and in miseries. — *William Shakespeare*

OPTIMIST

AN optimist sees an opportunity in every calamity. A pessimist sees a calamity in every opportunity. — *Herbert V. Prochnow*

OPTIMIST

AN optimist does not simply think of his success, he lives it.

— Maurice D. Sachnoff

ORIGINALITY

BE the first to say what is self-evident, and you are immortal.

— M. Ebner-Eschenbach

OTHERS

HE who does nothing for others does nothing for himself. *— Goethe*

THE more we help others, the more closely we touch other lives, the more we expand and grow ourselves, the more love and power comes back to us. *— O.S. Marden*

PAIN

THERE is no real ill in life except severe bodily pain; everything else is the child of the imagination; all other ills find a remedy, either from time, or moderation, or strength of mind. *— Marie de Sevigne*

PAIN is man's kindest benefactor, often revealing to him his plight in time to apply a remedy. *— Alfred A. Montapert*

PARENT

THERE is no friendship, no love, like that of the parent for the child. *— Henry Ward Beecher*

SPEAKING personally, I have found the happiness of parenthood greater than any other I have experienced. *— Bertrand Russell*

PASSION

MANY are slaves of their own passions. They do not have control of themselves. They spend most of their lives pecking and crowing with the chickens. Life passes them by. — *Alfred A. Montapert*

WHATEVER makes the passions pure, makes them stronger, more durable, and more enjoyable. — *Joseph Joubert*

HAPPY is he who is engaged in controversy with his own passions and comes off superior; who makes it his endeavor that his follies and weaknesses may die before himself, and who daily meditates on morality and immortality. — *John Jortin*

PAST

FOUR things come not back: the spoken word, the sped arrow, the past, the neglected opportunity. — *Omar Idn Al-Halif*

PATIENCE

The first rules of life you learn in later years ... everything takes longer than you think it's going to. — *Alfred A. Montapert*

THERE is no road too long to the man who advances deliberately and without undue haste; no honors too distant to the man who prepares himself for them with patience. — *Jean de La Bruyere*

A PATIENT mind is the best remedy for trouble. — *Titus Maccius Plautus*

PATIENCE is not passive; on the contrary it is active; it is concentrated strength. — *Edward Bulwer-Lytton*

PATIENCE

PATIENCE and perseverance have a magical effect before which difficulties disappear and obstacles vanish. — *John Quincy Adams*

MEN lack patience and persistence more than talent. — *Anonymous*

IF you are patient in one moment of anger, you will escape one hundred days of sorrow. — *Chinese Proverb*

PATRIOTISM

IN peace patriotism really consists only in this . . . that everyone sweeps before his own door, minds his own business, also learns his own lesson, that it may be well with him in his own house. — *Goethe*

THINK rather of performing your duties than of claiming your rights. — *John Lubbock*

AND so, my fellow Americans, ask not what your country can do for you. Ask what you can do for your country. — *John F. Kennedy*

PAY

A MAN is not paid for having a head and hands, but for using them. — *Elbert G. Hubbard*

PEACE

TO be prepared for war is one of the most effectual means of preserving peace. — *George Washington*

COME unto me, all ye that labor and are heavy laden, and I will give you rest. — *Matthew 11:28*

PEACE

PEACE comes from within. Do not seek it without.   — *Buddha*

PEACE OF MIND

TO be good company for ourselves we must store our minds well; fill them with pure and peaceful thoughts; with pleasant memories of the past, and reasonable hopes for the future.   — *Alfred A. Montapert*

REAL wealth is NOT from an abundance of worldly goods but from a contented mind.   — *Alfred A. Montapert*

A MAN finds peace in the work of the spirit.   — *Bhagavad-Gita*

PEOPLE

FORMULA FOR HANDLING PEOPLE:
    1. Listen to the other person's story.
    2. Listen to the other person's full story.
    3. Listen to the other person's full story first.
          — *General George C. Marshall*

THE wisest man I have ever known once said to me, "Nine out of every ten people improve on acquaintance," and I have found his words to be true.   — *Frank Swinnerton*

PEOPLE can be placed in three classes: the few who make things happen; the many who watch things happen; and the overwhelming majority who have no idea of what has happened. We need more people who make things happen.   — *Nicholas M. Butler*

ASSETS make things possible, but people make them happen.
          — *Alfred A. Montapert*

PERFECTION

TRIFLES make perfection, but perfection is no trifle.

— Michelangelo

PERFECTION consists not in doing extraordinary things, but in doing ordinary things extraordinarily well.

— A. Arnauld

AIM at perfection in everything, though in most things it is unattainable. However, they who aim at it, and persevere, will come much nearer to it than those whose laziness and despondency will make them give it up as unattainable. *— Lord Chesterfield*

HE who boasts of being perfect is perfect in folly. I never saw a perfect man. Every rose has its thorns, and every day its night. Even the sun shows spots, and the skies are darkened by clouds. And faults of some kind nestle in every bosom. *— Charles H. Spurgeon*

PERFORMANCE

EACH honest calling, each walk of life, has its own aristocracy based on excellence of performance. *— James Conant*

WHAT makes the difference between man and man is real performance, and not genius or conception. *— Thomas Gainsborough*

PERSEVERANCE/PERSISTENCE

IF you start to take Vienna . . . take Vienna. *— Napoleon Bonaparte*

THROUGH perseverance many people win success out of what seemed destined to be certain failure. *— Benjamin Disraeli*

Be of good cheer. Do not think of today's failures, but of the success that may come tomorrow. You have set yourselves a difficult task, but you will succeed if you persevere; and you will find a joy in overcoming obstacles. Remember, no effort that we make to attain something beautiful is ever lost.
— *Helen Keller*

NOTHING in the world can take the place of persistence. Talent will not; nothing is more common than unsuccessful men with talent. Genius will not; unrewarded genius is almost a proverb. Education will not; the world is full of educated derelicts. Persistence and determination alone are omnipotent. The slogan "Press On" has solved and always will solve the problems of the human race.
— *Calvin Coolidge*

PERSONALITY

MAKE the most of yourself, for that is all there is to you.
— *Ralph Waldo Emerson*

THE strange and wonderful thing is that you establish in the very atmosphere around you a vibration that is felt by everyone who comes near you.
— *Eric Butterworth*

PERSPECTIVE

TRY to see the unseen.
— *Alfred A. Montapert*

WE shall see but little way if we require to understand what we see. How few things can a man measure with the tape of his understanding! How many greater things might he be seeing in the meanwhile!
— *Henry David Thoreau*

TWO men look out through the self-same bars; one sees the mud, the other, the stars.
— *Frederick Langbridge*

PERSUASION

THE people understand only what they feel; the only orators that can affect them are those who move them. — *Lamartine*

FEW are open to conviction, but the majority of men are open to persuasion. — *Goethe*

ADVERTISING is persuasion, and persuasion is an art, not a science. — *Bill Bernbach*

PESSIMIST

PESSIMISTS are seldom disappointed. — *William D. Montapert*

PHILOSOPHY

PHILOSOPHY ... is not theology, for where theology takes its departure from articles of religious faith, philosophy starts with common sense and attempts to refine and deepen the understanding of the world which is latent in common sense. — *Mortimer J. Adler*

A MAN without a philosophy is a man without LIFE. To put more LIFE in your LIVING you have to develop a HEALTHY PHILOSO-PHY to chart your course through LIFE. — *Alfred A. Montapert*

A LITTLE philosophy inclineth a man's mind to atheism ... but depth in philosophy bringeth men's minds to God. — *Sir Francis Bacon*

THE world is my country, all mankind are my brethren. And to do good is my religion. — *Thomas Paine*

MY PHILOSOPHY ... I keep in line with the word of God and do MY BEST ... God will do the rest. — *Alfred A. Montapert*

PLAN

MOST misery and troubles can be traced to lack of wise planning and right thinking beforehand. — *Anthony B. Montapert*

VERY few know how to manage time, life, and motivate themselves. People do not plan to fail . . . they fail to plan. — *Alfred A. Montapert*

A MAN who does not plan long ahead will find trouble right at his door. — *Confucius*

AN intelligent plan is the first step to success. The man who plans knows where he is going, knows what progress he is making and has a pretty good idea when he will arrive. Planning is the open road to your destination. If you don't know where you are going, how can you expect to get there? — *Basil Walsh*

ALWAYS remember . . . THE BEST IS YET TO BE . . . if you PLAN for it. — *Alfred A. Montapert*

PLAY

WHEN you play, play with all your might, but when you work, don't play at all. — *Theodore Roosevelt*

PLAY and joking should have a certain natural delight, but their frequent use deprives the mind of weight, and of all force. — *Seneca*

PLEASE

IT is a very hard undertaking to please everybody. — *Publilius Syrus*

HE who trims himself to suit everyone will soon whittle himself away. — *Raymond Hull*

PLEASURES

PLEASURE must not, nay, cannot, be the business of a man of sense and character; but it may be, and is, his relief, his reward.
— *Lord Chesterfield*

OF all pleasure, the fruit of labor is the sweetest.   — *Vauvenargues*

THAT man is the richest whose pleasures are the cheapest.
— *Henry David Thoreau*

I KNOW what pleasure is, for I have done good work.
— *Robert Louis Stevenson*

ENJOY present pleasures in such a way as not to injure future ones.
— *Seneca*

A MAN should hear a little music, read a little poetry, and cultivate good thoughts every day of his life, in order that worldly cares may not obliterate the sense of the beautiful which God has planted in the human soul.   — *Goethe*

YOUR greatest pleasure is that which rebounds from the hearts that you have made glad.   — *Henry Ward Beecher*

POETRY

WOULD you have your songs endure? Build on the human heart.
— *Robert Browning*

THE best words in the best order.   — *Samuel T. Coleridge*

A POEM begins in delight and ends in wisdom.   — *Robert Frost*

POETS and artists are the voices of the heart and soul which bring beauty . . . love . . . happiness.   — *Alfred A. Montapert*

POISE

CULTIVATE poise. It is power under control.   — *Grenville Kleiser*

POLITENESS

POLITENESS is an easy virtue, and has great purchasing power.
— *A.B. Alcott*

CEREMONIES are different in every country; but true politeness is everywhere the same.   — *Oliver Goldsmith*

TRUE politeness is perfect ease and freedom; it simply consists in treating others just as you love to be treated yourself.
— *Lord Chesterfield*

POLITICIANS

HE serves his party best . . . who serves the country best.
— *Rutherfield B. Hayes*

WHENEVER a man has cast a longing eye on offices, a rottenness begins in his conduct.   — *Thomas Jefferson*

POSSESSIONS

I HAVE held many things in my hands, and I have lost them all; but whatever I have placed in God's hands, that I still possess.
— *Martin Luther*

ALL our possessions are as nothing compared to health, strength, and a clear conscience.   — *Hosea Ballou*

A MAN'S life consisteth not in the abundance of the things he possesseth.   — *Luke 12:15*

NO man can lose what he never had.   — *Isaak Walton*

POSSIBILITY

MAKE the most of yourself by fanning the tiny spark of possibility within you into the flame of achievement.   — *Wilfred A. Peterson*

OUR aspirations are our possibilities.   — *Robert Browning*

POTENTIAL

FEW of us know what we are capable of doing . . . we have never pushed ourselves hard enough to find out.   — *Alfred A. Montapert*

DEVELOP your FULL POTENTIAL. No one but you can know what you can do, nor will you know until you have tried. — *Unknown*

THERE is nothing in a caterpillar that tells you it's going to be a butterfly. Who knows what MAN can become?   — *Buckminster Fuller*

POVERTY

POVERTY . . . is life near the bone, where it is sweetest.
          — *Henry David Thoreau*

POOR in purse, sick at heart.   — *Goethe*

POWER

ELECTRICITY is the Natural Power in the Natural Realm . . . The HOLY SPIRIT is GOD'S POWER in the Spiritual Realm. POWER does not do the job by itself, it must be governed. In the Human Realm MAN must mix his FAITH with the Higher Power to effect miracles . . . just as you pour two chemicals into the one jar to cause an explosion.   — *Alfred A. Montapert*

THERE was a certain power in Lincoln and Washington greater than their words.   — *Ralph Waldo Emerson*

THE Cross I bear is Power.   — *Victor Hugo*

GOD'S POWER

MIGHTY FAITH makes the heart full of the POWER OF GOD. The only limit to the POWER OF GOD lies within YOU!

— *Alfred A. Montapert*

BUT they that wait upon the Lord shall renew their strength; they shall mount up with wings as eagles; they shall run, and not be weary; and they shall walk, and not faint.   — *Isaiah 40:31*

HIGHER POWER

DEEP within our consciousness is the realization there is a Higher Power . . . our Lord and God. That our life has a purpose, a destiny, a meaning, a relationship which must be discovered and developed. Until this is achieved you will experience boredom, frustration, dissatisfaction. Only the indwelling presence of this Power will satisfy the hunger of your soul.   — *Alfred A. Montapert*

LOOKING up at the heavens and contemplating the stars, what could be more obvious or clear than that some power of Superior Intelligence exists that controls all these things.   — *Cicero*

THINGS go better when we are in harmony with —
   The Divine Power that governs the universe . . .
   The Supreme Power that governs Nature . . .
   The Unseen Power that heals Mankind . . .
   The Almighty Power that gives abundant LIFE and LOVE.
In THIS POWER we live, move and have our being.

— *Alfred A. Montapert*

HIGHER POWER

AMONG the mysteries which become more mysterious the more they are thought about, there will remain the one absolute certainty that we are ever in the presence of an Infinite Power from which all things proceed. — *Herbert Spencer*

WE live in a universe of law and order. This means the forces that guide the planets are governed by a dependable Supreme Power. We can predict the appearance of a comet fifty years hence, for the laws that govern the universe are so dependable and accurate.
— *The Supreme Philosophy of Man*

PRACTICE

LET every man practice the art that he knows best. — *Cicero*

PRACTICE makes perfect. — *German Adage*

PRAISE

PRAISE, like gold and diamonds, owes its value only to its scarcity.
— *Samuel Johnson*

MANY men know how to flatter, few men know how to praise.
— *Greek Adage*

PRAYER

ONE prays as one loves, with one's whole being. — *Alexis Carrel*

PRAY to God, at the beginning of all thy works, that so thou mayest bring them all to a good ending. — *Xenophon*

YOU pray in your distress and in your need; would that you might pray also in the fullness of your joy and in your days of abundance.
— *Kahlil Gibran*

PRAYER

WE should pray for: Health enough to make work a pleasure; Strength enough to battle with difficulties and overcome them; Patience enough to toil until the most worthwhile good is accomplished; Love enough to make them most useful to others; Faith enough to make real the things of God; And hope enough to remove all anxieties concerning the future. *— Goethe*

THE key to the art of prayer is thought. As we think, so we pray. The highest level of prayer is to think God's thoughts after Him, to attune our lives to love, hope, faith, justice, kindness; to become open channels for the goodness of God. *— Wilfred A. Peterson*

PRAYER opens doors to let in God and let out self, to let in love and let out hate, to let in faith and let out fear. *— Wilfred A. Peterson*

HE prayeth best who loveth best. *— Samuel T. Coleridge*

DESIRE is prayer. Work is prayer. Thinking is prayer. Decision is faith and prayer. *— Stella T. Mann*

HAPPY is the man who has learned the secret of coming to God daily in prayer. Fifteen minutes alone with God every morning before you start the day can change circumstances and remove mountains. *— Billy Graham*

THE need of God expresses itself in prayer. Prayer is a cry of distress; a demand for help; a hymn of love. *— Alexis Carrel*

MORE things are wrought by prayer than this world dreams of. *— Alfred Lord Tennyson*

PRAYER is the contemplation of the facts of life from the highest point of view. *— Ralph Waldo Emerson*

PRAY for a good harvest . . . but keep on plowing. *— Anonymous*

PRAYER

THROUGH prayer and meditation we allow entry into ourselves of the deeper streams of life, and are compensated with serenity, peace of mind and joy. — *Alfred A. Montapert*

DO you wish to find out the really sublime? Repeat the Lord's Prayer. — *Napoleon Bonaparte*

HE is a FOOL who tries to live in a world like this without prayer . . . What an empty void life at once becomes when we have no fellowship with the Infinite . . . when we lose the art of prayer.

— *A.P. Gouthey*

EVERY time you pray, if your prayer is sincere, there will be new feeling and new meaning in it which will give you fresh courage, and you will understand that prayer is an education. — *Fyodor Dostoyevski*

PRAYER is talking to God. MEDITATION is listening for his answer.

— *Anonymous*

IT isn't the words that we utter in prayer that count . . . it is the FAITH which the heart of us exercises that gets results.

— *Alfred A. Montapert*

LET the words of my mouth and the meditation of my heart be acceptable in Thy sight, O Lord, my strength, and my Redeemer.

— *Psalm 19:14*

PRECEDE

COMING events cast their shadows before them. — *Thomas Campbell*

PREDICTIONS

THE two hardest things in the world to predict are the WEATHER and PEOPLE. — *Alfred A. Montapert*

PREPARATION

IF I had eight hours to chop down a tree, I'd spend six sharpening my ax.
— *Abraham Lincoln*

IF thou art not prepared today, how wilt thou be tomorrow?
— *Anonymous*

PRESENT

OUR great business in life is not to see what lies dimly at a distance, but to do what lies clearly at hand.
— *Thomas Carlyle*

WHAT use we make of the present will determine how the future will use us.
— *A.P. Gouthey*

HE lives twice who can at once employ the present well, and then the past enjoy.
— *Alexander Pope*

EVERY man's life lies within the present; for the past is spent and done with, and the future is uncertain.
— *Marcus Aurelius*

TAKE care of the present and the future will take care of itself.
— *Hanford L. Gordon*

HOW quickly will pass this PRESENT. How soon each one of us shall have done with the things which we have, and handle. How soon we shall be called to recognize the fullest extent of GOD's amazing provision for us.
— *Alfred A. Montapert*

PREVENTION

IT is less costly to service a machine properly than to mend it after it breaks down ... the Human Machine as well as all others, both electrical and mechanical.
— *Alfred A. Montapert*

PREVENTION is the best cure.
— *Proverb*

PRICE

THERE is hardly anything in the world that someone cannot make a little worse and sell a little cheaper, and the people who consider price only are this man's lawful prey. — *John Ruskin*

THE quality of our work and products remain long after the price has been forgotten. — *Alfred A. Montapert*

PRIDE

YOU'VE got to have pride. Pride is what makes a winning performance. If two teams are the same in physical ability and mental ability, it's the team with pride that wins.
— *Vince Lombardi*

PRIDE knows no pain. — *Richard W. Sampson*

PRINCIPLES

ONE may be better than his reputation or his conduct, but never better than his principles. — *Latena*

NEVER compromise a principle or relinquish a vital truth.
— *Alfred A. Montapert*

PRINCIPLE is a passion for truth and right. — *William Hazlitt*

IF we work marble, it will perish; if we work upon brass, time will efface it; if we rear temples, they will crumble into dust; but if we work upon immortal minds and instill in them just principles, we are then engraving upon them tablets which no time will efface, but will brighten and brighten to all eternity. — *Daniel Webster*

PROBLEMS

IF all our misfortunes were laid in one common heap, whence everyone must take an equal portion, most people would be content to take their own and depart. — *Socrates*

EXPECT problems and learn to eat them for breakfast.
— *Alfred A. Montapert*

A PROBLEM well stated is a problem half-solved. State the problem well . . . and you are half-way there. — *Charles F. Kettering*

IF you cannot RECOGNIZE . . . IDENTIFY and TALK about a problem, you cannot solve it. And if you cannot solve a problem you cannot succeed. — *Alfred A. Montapert*

PROBLEMS are only opportunities in work clothes. — *Henry J. Kaiser*

WITH God all things are possible! Have FAITH . . . DIFFICUL-TIES, PROBLEMS, CHALLENGES are the names given to the things which it is our business to overcome. — *Alfred A. Montapert*

I'VE been in the inventor business for many years and my experience is that for every problem we face, the Lord has made a solution.
— *Thomas Alva Edison*

THE happiest people are not the people without problems . . . they are the people who know how to solve their problems.
— *Robert Schuller*

PROCRASTINATION

PROCRASTINATION is the thief of time. — *Edward Young*

IF you wait too long to make a decision, you are not making a decision at all. You are avoiding one. — *Anonymous*

PRODUCTIVITY

UNLESS man produces more than he receives, increases his output, there will be less for him and all the others. — *Bernard Baruch*

MASS production precedes mass consumption and makes it possible, by reducing cost and thus permitting both greater use-convenience and price-convenience. — *Henry Ford*

THE day is approaching when we shall learn to estimate the importance of man not by his income, but by his output. They call it PRODUCTIVITY. — *Alfred A. Montapert*

PROFIT

THE proof of the pudding is in the profit. — *Anonymous*

IN business the earning of profit is something more than an incident of success. It is an essential condition of success; because the continued absence of profit itself spells failure. — *Louis Brandeis*

IF you count all of your assets you will always show a profit. — *Alfred A. Montapert*

PROGRESS

IN the final analysis, there is no other solution to man's progress but the day's honest work, the day's honest activities, the day's generous utterances and the day's good deeds. — *Clare Boothe Luce*

MAN can know more than their ancestors did if they start with a knowledge of what their ancestors had already learned. That is why a society can be progressive only if it conserves its tradition. — *Walter Lippman*

BEHOLD the turtle. He makes progress only when he sticks his neck out.
— *James B. Conant*

DO not confuse motion with progress. A rocking-horse keeps moving but does not make any progress.
— *Alfred A. Montapert*

PROGRESS always involves risk. You can't steal second base and keep your foot on first.
— *Frederick B. Wilcox*

CHANGE does not necessarily assure progress, but progress implacably requires change. Education is essential to change, for education creates both wants and the ability to satisfy them.
— *Henry Steele Commager*

IT is in the realm of uncertainties that progress, if it is ever to be encountered, must lie.
— *Edward Searles*

TO change and change for the better are two different things.
— *German Proverb*

PROMISE

NEVER promise more than you can perform.
— *Publilius Syrus*

BAD promises are better broken than kept.
— *Abraham Lincoln*

HE who is slow in promising is always the most faithful in performing.
— *Jean Jacques Rousseau*

PROSPERITY

PROSPERITY is a state of mind which enhances every area of living: HEALTH . . . WEALTH . . . HAPPINESS. Every day YOU write your own paycheck!
— *Alfred A. Montapert*

HE that tilleth his land shall be satisfied with bread: but he that followeth vain persons is void of understanding.
— *Proverbs 12:11*

PROVERBS

A PROVERB is a short sentence based on long experience.

— Miguel de Cervantes

DESPISE not the discoveries of the wise, but acquaint thyself with their proverbs for of them thou shalt learn instruction. *— Apocrypha*

A SHORT saying often contains much wisdom. *— Sophocles*

WISDOM lies in proverbs, which are brief and pithy. Collect and learn them ... You have much in little; they save time in speaking; and upon occasions may be the fullest and safest answer.

— William Penn

PRUDENCE

CHANCE fights ever on the side of the prudent. *— Euripides*

A FOOL despiseth his father's instruction; but he that regardeth reproof is prudent. *— Proverbs 15:5*

PSYCHIATRY/PSYCHOLOGY

PSYCHIATRY fails to utilize the great store of wisdom that can be found in religious admonitions. "Do not blame them, for they know not what they do." This is of greater value in eliminating inferiority and guilt complexes than all of Freud's distorted theories about man and life. *— A.P. Gouthey*

PSYCHOLOGY alone is never enough for man's greatest adventure ... life! Like all other sciences, it formulates no moral goal; it is not a philosophy of life, nor did its pioneers ever intend it to be. It is a key to the temple, not the temple itself. *— Joshua Liebman*

PSYCHIATRIST

THERE'S nothing wrong with the average person that a good psychiatrist can't exaggerate. — *Toronto Star*

PUNISHMENT

EVERY great example of punishment has in it some injustice; but the suffering individual is compensated by the public good. — *Tacitus*

WICKEDNESS, when properly punished, is disgraceful only to the offender; unpunished, it is disgraceful to the whole community.
— *Charles Simmons*

WE are not punished for our sins but by them. — *Elbert G. Hubbard*

HE who does not punish evil commands it to be done.
— *Leonardo da Vinci*

PURPOSE

PURPOSE is what gives life its meaning. — *C.H. Parkhurst*

SOME men have a purpose in life, and some have none. Our first object should be to make the most and best of ourselves.
— *John Lubbock*

I ALWAYS have to be sure I help and edify people, for that's my name on the book. — *Alfred A. Montapert*

QUALITY

CREAM always rises to the top. — *Anonymous*

QUALITY

A BIG, spectacular thing can frequently be accomplished quickly. Quality usually takes longer. Fanfare and fireworks are not part of quality; therefore, only those who know true values are attracted to it. But when the fanfare and fireworks are over, quality will remain.

— *Alfred A. Montapert*

I AM easily satisfied with the best.   — *Sir Winston Churchill*

QUEST

LIFE'S most successful quest is putting oneself in second place . . . God in the first. All else in life bends to this.   — *Alfred A. Montapert*

QUESTION

MAN has made some machines that can answer questions provided the facts are profusely stored in them, but we will never be able to make a machine that will ask questions. The ability to ask the right question is more than half the battle of finding the answer.

— *Thomas J. Watson*

"HOW do you know so much about everything?" was asked of a very wise and intelligent man. And the answer was, "By never being afraid or ashamed to ask questions as to anything of which I was ignorant."   — *Anonymous*

IF you do not ask the right question, you do not get the right answers. A question asked in the right way often points to its own answer. Asking questions is the A-B-C of diagnosis. Only the inquiring mind solves problems.   — *Edward Hodnett*

WHAT do I really want? This is one of the most important questions you will ever ask yourself. Spell out your desires.

— *Alfred A. Montapert*

QUIET

IT is the seed of quiet, and its fruit, that helps to develop a strong personality that can stand up masterfully to all kinds of pressure.
— *L.R. Ditzen*

A MAN that will enjoy a quiet conscience must lead a quiet life.
— *Lord Chesterfield*

SOLITUDE and concentration . . . are a must for our best thinking.
— *Alfred A. Montapert*

QUOTATIONS

TO quote copiously and well requires taste, judgment and erudition, a feeling for the beautiful, an appreciation of the noble, and a sense of the profound.
— *Christian N. Bovee*

EVERYTHING of importance has been said before by somebody who did not discover it.
— *Alfred North Whitehead*

THE wisdom of the wise and the experience of the ages are perpetuated by quotation.
— *Benjamin Disraeli*

I QUOTE others only in order the better to express myself.
— *Michel de Montaigne*

A COLLECTION of rare thoughts is nothing less than a cabinet of intellectual gems.
— *W. H. Sprague*

THE next thing to saying a good thing yourself, is to quote one. All minds quote.
— *Ralph Waldo Emerson*

HE that lays down precepts for the governing of our lives and moderating our passions, obliges humanity, not only in the present, but in all future generations.
— *Seneca*

READINESS

NO man is worth his salt who is not ready at all times to risk his body, his well-being, his life in a great cause.

— *Theodore Roosevelt*

READING

A GOOD reader is nearly as rare as a good writer.

— *Robert E. A. Willmott*

TO read without reflecting is like eating without digesting.

— *Edmund Burke*

A CAPACITY and taste for reading gives access to whatever has been discovered by others. It is the key, or one of the keys, to the already solved problems. And not only so; it gives a relish and facility for successfully pursuing the unsolved ones. — *Abraham Lincoln*

IN reading, we hold converse with the wise; in the business of life, generally with the foolish. — *Sir Francis Bacon*

READING books in one's youth is like looking at the moon through a crevice; reading books in middle age is like looking at the moon in one's courtyard; and reading books in old age is like looking at the moon on an open terrace. This is because depth of benefits of reading varies in proportion to the depth of one's own experience.

— *Chang Ch'ao*

THE wise man reads both books and life itself. — *Lin Yutang*

PEOPLE say that life is the thing, but I prefer reading.

— *Logan Pearsall Smith*

READING

READ the preface first, go in through the front door. Read the old books . . . those that have stood the test of time. Read them slowly, carefully, thoroughly. They will help you to discriminate among the new ones. Read plenty of books about people and things, but not too many books about books. Read one book at a time, but never one book alone. Well-born books have relatives. Follow them up.

— Henry Van Dyke

I LOVE to lose myself in other men's minds.   *— Charles Lamb*

READING maketh a full man, conference a ready man, writing an exact man.   *— Sir Francis Bacon*

I AM a part of all that I have read.   *— John Kieran*

THE person who acquires the habit of intelligent reading invariably gets more out of life. Books kindle the imagination and enrich the whole being with grace and power.   *— Alfred A. Montapert*

BE careful what you read . . . for you become what you dwell upon.

— Alfred A. Montapert

REALITY

REALITY is NOT the way you wish things to be, but the way they actually are. To be happy we must face REALITY.

— Alfred A. Montapert

IT is essential to base oneself, not on the visions of the mind, but on the results of observation and experience.   *— Alexis Carrel*

LIFE'S experiences are intended to make you eventually face yourself. Face reality!   *— Harold Sherman*

RECORD

NOT one of us has a blank page in the books of the Recording Angel.
— *George Bernard Shaw*

RECREATION

HE that will make a good use of any part of his life must allow a large part of it for recreation. — *John Locke*

GAMES give moral, as well as physical, health; daring and endurance, self-command and good humor, qualities which are not to be found in books, and no teaching can give. — *John Lubbock*

RED

AS for me, I would rather be dead than Red. — *J. Edgar Hoover*

REFLECTION

IN the rush of youth, we find little time or inclination to meditate and reflect, but, as we grow older, we like to recall our many experiences, study and weigh them, and thereby gain at least some little measure of that wonderful quality called wisdom . . . a product of accumulated experience, knowledge, and reflection — *William Ross*

EDUCATION begins the gentleman, but reading, good company, and reflection must finish him. — *John Locke*

REFLECT upon your present blessings, of which every man has many; not on your past misfortunes, of which all men have some.
— *Charles Dickens*

IT is a most mortifying reflection for a man to consider what he has done, compared with what he might have done. — *Samuel Johnson*

RELAXATION

SOME relaxation is necessary to people of every degree; the head that thinks and the hand that labors, must have some little time to recruit their diminished powers.
— *Bernard Gilpin*

RELAXED attitudes are the means towards the GREATEST HAPPI-NESS as well as the greatest EFFICIENCY in life. Make sure you take time out (now and then) to FISH and THINK, and you will learn Serenity, and HOW TRANSITORY are human affairs.
— *Michel de Montaigne*

LEARN to relax. Great tension is an abomination. The more tense we become, the more stupidly we are likely to act. Today many so-called efficient people are perpetually on the verge of a nervous breakdown. You are a better producer and a better provider if you do not collapse from psychic exhaustion at some critical moment, when you are most in need of good health.
— *Alfred A. Montapert*

RELIGION

THE strength of a country is the strength of its religious convictions.
— *Calvin Coolidge*

RELIGION is the tie that connects man with his Creator.
— *Daniel Webster*

NO sciences are better attested than the religion of the Bible.
— *Sir Isaac Newton*

RELIGION is the first thing and the last thing, and until a man has found God and been found by God, he begins at no beginning and he works to no end.
— *H. G. Wells*

HONOR . . . HONESTY . . . INTEGRITY . . . are the primary MORAL and ETHICAL teachings of every religion.
— *Alfred A. Montapert*

RELIGION

THIS is what I found out about religion: It gives you courage to make the decisions you must make in a crisis, and then the confidence to leave the result to Higher Power. Only by trust in God can a man carrying responsibility find repose. — *Dwight D. Eisenhower*

MANY have quarreled about religion who never practiced it.
— *Benjamin Franklin*

RELIGION is the light of our life, Faith is the key that turns it on.
— *Tennessee Ernie Ford*

RELIGION holds the solution to all problems of human relationship, whether they are between parents and children or nation and nation. Sooner or later, man has always had to decide whether he worships his own power or the power of God. — *Arnold Toynbee*

THE religions of the world must be appreciated for what they were and are ... living things, impulses to worship, commanding man's most passionate feeling and dedication, carrying him beyond himself, engaging his deepest commitments and loyalties.
— *Alfred A. Montapert*

REMEDY

THERE is a remedy for every wrong, and a satisfaction for every soul. — *Ralph Waldo Emerson*

TO do nothing is sometimes a good remedy. — *Hippocrates*

PATIENCE is the best remedy for every trouble. — *Plautus*

A DOCTOR'S ability cannot be accurately judged when his diagnosis and prescribed remedy is rejected ... or neglected. — *A.P. Gouthey*

A REMEDY against all ills ... poverty, sickness, and melancholy ... only one thing is absolutely necessary: a liking for work.
— *Charles Baudelaire*

REPUTATION

YOU cannot build a reputation on what you are going to do.
— *Henry Ford*

IT is of very little account what men think of us, but it is of great importance what God thinks of us. — *D. L. Moody*

RESEARCH

BASIC research is what I am doing when I don't know what I'm doing. — *Wernher von Braun*

RESEARCH is an organized method for keeping you reasonably dissatisfied with what you have. — *Charles Kettering*

RESEARCH serves to make building stones out of stumbling blocks.
— *Arthur D. Little*

RESOURCES

IT is at least something to know that when one is thrown on one's own resources, one learns then to use them properly.
— *Sigmund Freud*

FEW men during their lifetime come anywhere near exhausting the resources dwelling within them. There are deep wells of strength that are never used. — *Richard E. Byrd*

RESPECT

I DISAPPROVE of what you say, but I will defend to the death your right to say it. — *Francois Voltaire*

THE youth fights that the old man may enjoy. — *Goethe*

RESPONSIBILITY

RESPONSIBILITIES gravitate to the person who can shoulder them; power flows to the man who knows how. — *Elbert G. Hubbard*

GOD gives us three score and ten years. All over is PROFIT . . . if we don't "screw up" or "burn out." — *Alfred A. Montapert*

RESPONSIBILITY is the thing people dread most of all. Yet it is the one thing in the world that develops us. — *Dr. Frank Crane*

IN the long run, we shape our lives, and we shape ourselves. The process never ends until we die. And the choices we make are ultimately our own responsibility. — *Eleanor Roosevelt*

YOU cannot build character and courage by taking away a man's initiative and independence. You cannot help men permanently by doing for them what they could and should do for themselves.
— *Abraham Lincoln*

LIFE is the acceptance of responsibilities or their evasion; it is a business of meeting obligations or avoiding them. — *Unknown*

EACH OF US IS RESPONSIBLE FOR WHAT WE MAKE OF OUR OWN LIFE. The government cannot play God and create people who are identical in ability. This development is an INDIVIDUAL RESPONSIBILITY. — *Alfred A. Montapert*

THE plea of ignorance will never take away our responsibilities.
— *John Ruskin*

REST

NO rest is worth anything except the rest that is earned.
— *Jean Paul Richter*

THE idle man does now know what it is to rest. — *John Lubbock*

RESULTS

BEFORE every action ask yourself . . . Will this bring more monkeys on my back? Will the result of my action be a Blessing or a Heavy Burden? — *Alfred A. Montapert*

THE world is not interested in the storms you encountered, but did you bring in the ship? — *William McFee*

THERE is a vast difference between being busy and being fruitful. Some give the impression of working hard . . . but they are not accomplishing. Results are what life is all about. — *Alfred A. Montapert*

ON a number of office walls I have seen this slogan: 57 Rules for Success: 1. Get results. 2. It doesn't matter about the other 56. — *Charles Allen*

WHAT we are after is results. If the contractor prefers to mix his concrete in Haymarket Square and bring it up here in his hat, we are not concerned so long as when it is in place, it will answer our purposes. — *Charles Gow*

YOU get the best out of others when you give the best of yourself. — *Harvey Firestone*

IF you want anything done . . . go to a busy person. — *Old Saying*

RUSHING around smartly is no proof of accomplishing much. — *Mary Baker Eddy*

RETICENT

THE fellow who keeps his thoughts to himself is likely to have some. — *Anonymous*

LET another man praise thee, and not thine own mouth; a stranger, and not thine own lips. — *Proverbs 27:2*

RETIREMENT

A MAN who can retire from the world to seek entertainment in his closet has a thousand advantages of which other people have no idea. He is master of his own company and pleasures, and can command either the one or the other according to his circumstances or temper. All nature is ready for his view, and all ages appear at his call. He can transport himself to the most distant regions, and enjoy the best and politest company that ever the world afforded.

— Hibernicus's Letters

RETRIBUTION

WE must sleep in the beds we prepare for ourselves. Too little is said of the price we pay for our own folly.   *— Alfred A. Montapert*

WHOSO diggeth a pit shall fall therein; and he that rolleth a stone, it will return upon him.   *— Proverbs 26:27*

REVENGE

TIME spent in getting even would be better spent in getting ahead.

— Anonymous

I NEVER trouble to be avenged. When a man injures me, I put his name on a slip of paper and lock it up in a drawer. It is marvelous how the men I have thus labeled have the knack of disappearing.

— Benjamin Disraeli

REWARD

THERE is probably but one answer to the question, "What do we get out of life?" And that is, "We get out of life exactly what we put into it," but we get that back in great abundance.

— Alfred A. Montapert

THERE never was a person who did anything worth doing that did not receive more than he gave.   *— Henry Ward Beecher*

BE thou faithful unto death and I will give thee a crown of life.

— *Revelations 2:10*

IT is one of the most beautiful compensations of life that no man can sincerely try to help another without helping himself.

— *Ralph Waldo Emerson*

THE reward of a thing well done is to have done it.

— *Ralph Waldo Emerson*

THE highest reward for man's toil is not what he gets for it, but what he becomes by it. — *John Ruskin*

NO man was ever honored for what he received. Honor is the reward for what he gave. — *Woodrow Wilson*

WHATSOEVER a man soweth, that shall he also reap.

— *Galatians 6:7*

EVERY man shall have his own reward according to his own labor.

— *I Corinthians 3:8*

RICH/RICHES

LET a boy know that he is going to be rich when he grows up and in nine cases out of ten he will turn out worthless. — *Richard Sage*

A STEADY job is the best get-rich scheme in the world.

— *Roy L. Smith*

ONE of the happiest traits of character is to be rich without much money . . . rich in intellect, rich in ideas, rich in deeds, rich in health and happiness, rich in soul. Where is the millionaire that in nobility stands as an equal to a Gladstone, a Henry Wilson, or a Sumner?

— *H. F. Kletzing*

THE best condition in life is not to be so rich as to be envied nor so poor as to be damned. — *Josh Billings*

RICH/RICHES

IF you want to know how rich you really are, find out what would be left of you tomorrow if you should lose every dollar you own tonight.
— *W. J. Boetcker*

IF you do not desire much, little will seem much to you; for small wants give poverty the power of wealth. — *Democritus*

A SAVER grows rich by seeming poor. A spender grows poor by seeming rich. — *Anonymous*

YOU are affluent when you buy what you want, do what you wish, and don't give a thought to what it costs. — *J. P. Morgan*

THE rich are not always Godly . . . but the Godly are always rich!
— *Anonymous*

ONCE you are rich you are usually always rich. Money makes money. — *Alfred A. Montapert*

IT is better to live rich than to die rich. — *Samuel Johnson*

IT is the heart that makes a man rich. He is rich according to what he is . . . not according to what he has. — *Henry Ward Beecher*

HE who knows the most; he who knows what sweets and virtues are in the ground, the waters, the plants, the heavens, and how to come at these enchantments, is the rich and royal man.
— *Ralph Waldo Emerson*

RIGHT

LET a man try faithfully, manfully to be right, he will daily grow more and more right. It is at the bottom of the condition on which all men have to cultivate themselves. — *Thomas Carlyle*

KEEP true, never be ashamed of doing right; decide on what you think is right, and stick to it.   — *George Eliot*

I MUST stand with anybody that stands right, stand with him while he is right and part with him when he goes wrong. — *Abraham Lincoln*

MY concern is not whether God is on our side, my great concern is to be on God's side, for God is always right.   — *Abraham Lincoln*

RIGHTEOUSNESS

THE whole universe is geared to righteousness. — *Alfred A. Montapert*

THERE is nothing more certain than that evil brings evil upon itself. And that is one of the most encouraging laws in the universe. It spells the final elimination of evil. All evil has within itself the seeds of its own destruction. By the same law righteousness survives. It has within itself the power of its own perpetuation. The reason is both simple and obvious: Righteousness originates with and in God. As long as He is ... righteousness remains.   — *Alfred A. Montapert*

RIGHTS

EVERYONE is bound to assert his rights and resist their invasion by others.   — *Immanuel Kant*

ALL men are endowed by their Creator with certain inalienable rights; that among these are life, liberty, and the pursuit of happiness.

— *Thomas Jefferson*
Declaration Of Independence

THE great right of all, without which there is, in fact, no right, is the right of taking a part in the making of the laws by which we are governed.   — *William Cobbett*

RISK

WHERE there is much to risk, there is much to consider.

— Platenus

THE people I want to hear about are the people who take risks.

— Robert Frost

FORTUNE favors the brave. *— Terence*

THOSE who trust to chance must abide by the results of chance.

— Calvin Coolidge

SABBATH

THE Sunday is the core of our civilization, dedicated to thought and reverence. It invites to the noblest solitude and to the noblest society. *— Ralph Waldo Emerson*

SIX days shall work be done, but on the seventh day there shall be to you an holy day, a sabbath of rest to the Lord. *— Exodus 35:2*

SACRIFICE

HE who would accomplish little must sacrifice little. He who would achieve much must sacrifice much; he who would attain highly must sacrifice greatly. *— James Allen*

GIFTS and giving are not the first requisite to fellowship with God, but they are frequently the best proof of fellowship with Him. LOVE finds its supremest delight in giving, not in getting. Sacrifice is the best evidence of devotion. *— Alfred A. Montapert*

WHEN each of us reaches the end of what we are willing to sacrifice, we have reached the end of love. — *Alfred A. Montapert*

THERE can be no success without some sacrifice. — *Roy L. Smith*

SALESMAN

SALESMANSHIP requires, above all, the spirit of optimism.
— *Anonymous*

ASK people questions, it helps them to buy. — *Marchant*

PICTURE profits for the other fellow. He wants to know how he is going to benefit. Tell the man what he gets, not what you get.
— *Marchant*

EVERY great salesman has profoundly at heart the interest of his customer, and no business can develop except as it promotes the interest of those who use its goods or its services. — *Charles Schwab*

THE best alibi in the world is a signed order. — *Roy L. Smith*

SATISFACTION

THE solid satisfactions of life are won only through labor.
— *Charles Eliot*

NAUGHT but God can satisfy the soul. — *P. J. Bailey*

THE evening hours are the hours of satisfaction; to know that you have done a good day's work. — *Anonymous*

SATISFACTION lies in the EFFORT, not in the attainment.
— *Alfred A. Montapert*

SAVING

IF you want to know whether you are destined to be a success or failure in life, you can easily find out. The test is simple and infallible. Are you able to save money? If not, drop out, you will lose; the seed of success is not in you.   — *James J. Hill*

THE habit of saving is itself an education; it fosters every virtue, teaches self-denial, cultivates the sense of order, trains to forethought, and broadens the mind.   — *T.T. Munger*

A SLACK hand shows weakness; a tight hand, strength.
                                              — *Charles Buxton*

SAY

THERE are five things that can either make you or break you . . .
   1. What you say to other people
   2. What you say about other people
   3. What other people say to you
   4. What other people say about you
   5. What you say to yourself about yourself.   — *David Fink*

I HAVE never been hurt by anything I didn't say.   — *Calvin Coolidge*

BE ever on your guard what you say of any man, and to whom.
                                              — *Horace*

SCHOOLS

SCHOOL is but a mental gymnasium. The best thing a school can teach you is how to THINK for yourself. LOGICAL THINKING and GOOD LISTENING should become a way of life. IF YOU ARE NOT LISTENING, YOU ARE NOT LEARNING.
                                              — *Alfred A. Montapert*

OUR prisons are full and overflowing. Unless we teach Goodness, Character, Integrity, Discipline, Honesty and the generous qualities in the schools forthwith, our nation will end up in disaster, under the steamroller of intellectual mediocrity. — *Alfred A. Montapert*

SCIENCE

SCIENCE has to be understood in its broadest sense, as a method for apprehending all observable reality, and not merely as an instrument for acquiring specialized knowledge. — *Alexis Carrel*

THE science of today is the technology of tomorrow. — *Edward Teller*

ALL science has one aim, namely, to find a theory of nature.
— *Ralph Waldo Emerson*

THE real pleasure one gets out of science is to see what everybody else has seen before, but to think what no one else has ever thought.
— *Dr. Albert Szent Gyorgyi*

THE power of science and the responsibility of science have offered mankind a new opportunity not only for intellectual growth, but for moral discipline, not only for the acquisition of knowledge but for the strengthening of our nerves and our will. — *John F. Kennedy*

SCIENCE without religion is lame, religion without science is blind.
— *Albert Einstein*

THE work of science is to substitute facts for appearances, and demonstration for impressions. — *John Ruskin*

SCIENCE belongs to no one country. — *Louis Pasteur*

WHAT art was to the ancient world, science is to the modern.
— *Benjamin Disraeli*

SECRET

A TRULY wise man should have no keeper of his secret but himself.
— *Francois Guizot*

WHATEVER is known to thyself alone has always very great value.
— *Ralph Waldo Emerson*

THREE can keep a secret if two of them are dead.
— *Benjamin Franklin*

TO keep your secret is wisdom . . . but to expect others to keep it is folly.
— *Samuel Johnson*

A PURPOSE you impart is no longer your own.   — *Goethe*

SECURITY

THE only real security is in having a sense of God.
— *Alfred A. Montapert*

IF money is your hope for independence you will never have it. The only real security that a man can have in this world is a reserve of knowledge, experience and ability.   — *Henry Ford*

SEE

WHAT we are . . . that only can we see.   — *Ralph Waldo Emerson*

WHAT we see depends mainly on what we look for.   — *John Lubbock*

SEEK

ASK, and it shall be given you; seek, and ye shall find. — *Matthew 7:7*

SEEK ye first the Kingdom of God and HIS righteousness, and all these things shall be added unto you.   — *Matthew 6:33*

THE QUESTS OF LIFE are many and varied. Among them are the Quest of MONEY and POSSESSIONS, the Quest of LOVE, the Quest of TRUTH, the Quest of USEFULNESS and DUTY, the Quest of GOODNESS and of GOD, and the Quest of HAPPINESS and CONTENTMENT.   — Alfred A. Montapert

SELF

WHEN all is said, the greatest art is to limit and isolate one's self.
— Goethe

LET him that would save the world first move himself.   — Socrates

AN assertion of the self, a commitment, is essential if the self is to have any reality.   — Rollo May

THE greatest evils are from within us ... and from ourselves also we must look for our greatest good.   — Jeremy Taylor

A LIFE of so-called pleasure and self-indulgence is not a life of real happiness or true freedom.   — Alfred A. Montapert

LIVES are either self-centered or Christ-centered, and that factor determines well-being.   — Dr. George Truett

IN order to fulfill his Divine destiny, all that a man has to be is himself.   — Ernest Holmes

SELF-CONFIDENCE

SAY to yourself each morning ... "I will STRIVE today for ... HAPPINESS and HEALTH and SUCCESS!"   — Alfred A. Montapert

BELIEVE in yourself! Have faith in your abilities! Without a humble but reasonable confidence in your own powers you cannot be successful or happy.   — Norman Vincent Peale

SELF-CONFIDENCE

DO not attempt to do a thing unless you are sure of yourself; but do not relinquish it simply because someone else is not sure of you.
— *Stuart Edward White*

DARE only to believe in yourselves. — *Friedrich Nietzsche*

SELF-CONTROL

TEMPER, if ungoverned, governs the whole man.
— *Anthony Shaftesbury*

ANYBODY can become angry . . . that is easy; but to be angry with the right person, and to the right degree, and at the right time, and for the right purpose, and in the right way . . . that is not within everybody's power and is not easy. — *Aristotle*

I COUNT him braver who overcomes his desires than him who conquers his enemies; for the hardest victory is the victory over self.
— *Aristotle*

PRUDENT, cautious self-control is wisdom's root. — *Robert Burns*

THOUGH a man go out to battle a thousand times against a thousand men, if he conquers himself he is the greater conqueror. — *Buddha*

HE who reigns within himself and controls passions, desires and fears is more than a king. — *John Milton*

MAN is made or unmade by himself. For man to conquer himself . . . is the first and noblest victory. Man controls his own passions, emotions, future. Without self-control the good life is impossible.
— *Alfred A. Montapert*

NO man is free who is not master of himself. — *Epictetus*

SELF-DENIAL

MORE happiness is gained by self-denial than by self-indulgence. The senses, full of true delight as they are, will, if we yield to them, wreck us, like sirens of old, on the rocks and whirlpools of life.

— *John Lubbock*

LEARN HOW and WHEN to say NO ... for developing the power to say NO gives the capacity to say YES. — *Alfred A. Montapert*

ALL great virtues bear the imprint of self-denial. — *W. E. Channing*

SELF-DEVELOPMENT

THE greatest responsibility given to man is that of developing himself. Each individual must FAIL or SUCCEED strictly on his own. — *Alfred A. Montapert*

MAN'S main task in life is to give birth to himself, to become ... what he potentially is. — *Dr. Erich Fromm*

SELF-ESTEEM

IT is difficult to make a man miserable while he feels he is worthy of himself and claims kindred to the great God who made him.

— *Abraham Lincoln*

NO man can do anything well who does not esteem his work to be of importance. — *Ralph Waldo Emerson*

INSIST on yourself; never imitate. Your own gift you can present every moment with the cumulative force of a whole life's cultivation; but of the adopted talent of another you have only an extemporaneous half possession. — *Ralph Waldo Emerson*

SELF-ESTEEM

THINK highly of yourself, for the world takes you at your own estimate.
— *Anonymous*

ONE of the great lessons of life is for each individual to learn to be himself, to have confidence in the high impulses that come to him as an individual, and to know that a Power greater than he is has created him to be a little different from all the rest. — *Ernest Holmes*

PUBLIC opinion is a weak tyrant compared with our own private opinion. What a man thinks of himself, that it is which determines, or rather indicates, his fate.
— *Henry David Thoreau*

SELF-IMPROVEMENT

MAN cannot remake himself without suffering; for he is both marble and the sculptor.
— *Alexis Carrel*

THERE is no use whatever trying to help people who do not help themselves. You cannot push anyone up a ladder unless he be willing to climb himself.
— *Andrew Carnegie*

EMPLOY your time in improving yourself by other men's writings, so that you shall come more easily by what others have labored hard for.
— *Socrates*

SELF-KNOWLEDGE

WE know what we are, but not what we may be.
— *William Shakespeare*

SELF-reverence, self-knowledge, self-control. These three alone lead life to sovereign power.
— *Alfred Lord Tennyson*

THE unexamined life is not worth living.
— *Plato*

THE best-informed man is the one who knows himself.
— *Alfred A. Montapert*

ALTHOUGH men are accused for not knowing their own weakness, yet perhaps, as few know their own strength. It is in men as in soils, where sometimes there is a vein of gold which the owner knows not of.
— *Jonathan Swift*

MAKE it thy business to know thyself, which is the most difficult lesson in the world.
— *Miguel de Cervantes*

MAN is born a long way from himself. It takes a long time to "Know Thyself," some never do. He needs to see the end (eternal life) toward which he moves.
— *Alfred A. Montapert*

SELF-PITY

A SELF-pitying life is a doomed life. Only the life which deliberately picks up and starts over again is Victorious.
— *Alfred A. Montapert*

EVERYONE thinks his own burden heavy.
— *French Proverb*

SELF-RELIANCE

HE who serves himself has a good servant and a kind master.
— *Hanford L. Gordon*

POVERTY is uncomfortable, as I can testify; but nine times out of ten the best thing that can happen to a young man is to be tossed overboard and compelled to sink or swim for himself.
— *James Garfield*

THE man who makes a success of an important venture never waits for the crowd. He strikes out for himself. It takes nerve, it takes a lot of grit; but the man that succeeds has both.
— *C.V. White*

SELF-RELIANCE

MAN'S distinction is his determination to think for himself.
— *Hyman C. Rickover*

SELF-RESPECT

ONLY by self-respect will you compel others to respect you.
— *Fyodor Dostoyevski*

NO man can be happy within himself if he ever surrenders his dignity and self-respect. — *Alfred A. Montapert*

IF we do not believe in ourselves, how can we expect others to believe in us? — *Henry Miller*

UNLESS one builds on a foundation of self-respect, one's life structure, no matter how glittering and imposing on the outside, is corroded and honeycombed within, liable to collapse ignominiously at any moment. — *B. C. Forbes*

HE that respects himself is safe from others . . . he wears a coat of mail that none can pierce. — *Henry Wadsworth Longfellow*

SELFISHNESS

NO man can live happily who regards himself alone, who turns everything to his own advantage. You must live for another if you wish to live for yourself. — *Seneca*

NO man is more cheated than the selfish man. — *Henry Ward Beecher*

SELFISHNESS is the greatest curse of the human race.
— *William E. Gladstone*

SENSES

THE sense of taste is the most exquisite of all. — *Cicero*

COMMON SENSE

GOOD health and good sense are two of life's greatest blessings.
— *Publilius Syrus*

COMMON sense is the knack of seeing things as they are, and doing things as they ought to be done. — *C. E. Stowe*

COMMON sense is the genius of humanity. — *Goethe*

COMMON sense is nothing but the recognition of an orderly process in life . . . things move, unfold, and vary according to laws, rules, and inflexible bestowals or patterns from archetypes. — *Alfred A. Montapert*

SERMON

PERHAPS those who say they didn't get a thing out of the sermon didn't bring anything in which to take it home. — *N. A. Prichard*

THE best of all the preachers are the men who live their creeds.
— *Edgar A. Guest*

YOU can preach a better sermon with your life than with your lips.
— *Oliver Goldsmith*

A GOOD example is the best sermon. — *Benjamin Franklin*

A SONG will outlive all sermons in the memory. — *Henry Giles*

SERVICE

ONE of the most amazing things ever said on this earth is Jesus' statement: "He that is greatest among you shall be your servant." Nobody has one chance in a billion of being thought really great after a century has passed except those who have been the servants of all.
— *Harry E. Fosdick*

SERVICE

GOD'S objective is not to merely save us from wrong. His great concern is to secure our service for the right. — *A.P. Gouthey*

ONLY a life lived for others is a life worthwhile. — *Albert Einstein*

FROM our youth up most of us are taught to measure a man's success by what he is able to get from the world in wealth, honor and renown. The divine measure of the value of a man's life is not what he gets from the world, but what he gives to the world.
— *Alfred A. Montapert*

CHOOSE this day whom you will serve . . . But as for me and my house, we will serve the Lord. — *Joshua 24:15*

SHARING

SHARED joy is a double joy. Shared sorrow is half a sorrow.
— *Swedish Proverb*

SILENCE

THERE is no explanation quite so effective as silence. Explanations rarely explain. If you are right your life will do its own explaining. If you are wrong you can't explain. — *Alfred A. Montapert*

SILENCE does not indicate wisdom, knowing when to remain silent does. — *Frank Tyger*

DON'T speak unless . . . you can improve on the silence.
— *Spanish Saying*

SPEAKING dilutes your thinking. Keep silent and concentrate in order to get your most sublime ideas. Be SILENT until finally you begin to hear what the silence tells you. The small voice of silence often contains the greatest wisdom. To DREAM . . . to THINK . . . to KNOW . . . that is everything. — *Alfred A. Montapert*

THOUGHT works in silence, so does virtue.   — *Thomas Carlyle*

SILENCE and reserve suggest latent power. What some men think has more effect than what others say.   — *Lord Chesterfield*

THE finest command of language is often shown by saying nothing.
          — *Roger Babson*

WE are told ... that silence is golden. But not always. When protest is called for, silence is the cheapest, weakest kind of cowardice. When right and wrong is the issue, you will either speak out or be damned by your cowardice.   — *A.P. Gouthey*

SIMPLICITY

OUR life is frittered away by detail ... Simplicity, simplicity, simplicity!   — *Henry David Thoreau*

NOTHING is more simple than greatness; indeed, to be simple is to be great.   — *Ralph Waldo Emerson*

THE greatest truths are the simplest, and so are the greatest men.
          — *A.W. Hare*

IF you get simple beauty and naught else, you get about the best thing God invents.   — *Robert Browning*

SIMPLICITY is the badge of genius.   — *Alfred A. Montapert*

IN character, in manners, in style, in all things, the supreme excellence is simplicity.   — *Henry Wadsworth Longfellow*

SIMPLICITY is the key to the good life. Cut yourself away from the thousand little disturbances that steal your time. Be concerned over what you ARE ... not what you HAVE. YOUR VALUE is in YOURSELF. The more simple your life, the more likely you will move quietly across the path of years and free your mind and heart for those labors which are profitable in terms of growth.
          — *Alfred A. Montapert*

SIN

SIN is the violation of the LAWS OF THE UNIVERSE, the keeping of which makes for your highest good.   — *A. P. Gouthey*

MEN are punished by their sins, not for them.   — *Elbert G. Hubbard*

SIN is not hurtful because it is forbidden, but forbidden because it is hurtful.   — *Benjamin Franklin*

SIN is the refusal to submit to the order of things. Any act or thought which tends to diminish, disintegrate or destroy life in its specifically human expression is a sin.   — *Alexis Carrel*

SIN is not in the act, but in the choice.   — *John Ruskin*

THE first and worst of all frauds is to cheat oneself. All sin is easy after that.   — *J. Bailey*

IF thou wouldst conquer thy weakness thou must never gratify it. No man is compelled to evil; only his consent makes it his. It is no sin to be tempted; it is to yield and be overcome.   — *William Penn*

SIN writes histories; goodness is silent.   — *Goethe*

THE unpardonable sin is to shut God out of your life.
                                                    — *Alfred A. Montapert*

SINCERITY

SINCERITY, a deep, great, genuine sincerity, is the first characteristic of all men in any way heroic.   — *Thomas Carlyle*

SINCERITY is the highest compliment you can pay.
                                                    — *Ralph Waldo Emerson*

SINCERITY is to speak as we think, to do as we pretend and profess, to perform what we promise, and really to be what we would seem and appear to be.
— *John Tillotson*

SKEPTICISM

SKEPTICISM has never founded empires, established principles or changed the world's heart. The great doers in history have always been men of faith.
— *Edwin H. Chapin*

SLANDER

NO one is safe from slander. The best way is to pay no attention to it, but live in innocence and let the world talk.
— *Moliere*

SLEEP

SLEEP is a maker of makers.
— *Carl Sandburg*

WE sleep, but the loom of life never stops and the pattern which was weaving when the sun went down is weaving when it comes up tomorrow.
— *Henry Ward Beecher*

BETTER counsel comes overnight.
— *Gotthold E. Lessing*

IT is better to sleep on things beforehand, than to lie awake about them afterwards.
— *Baltasar Gracian*

SLOW

WE are losing our sense of leisure. In a frenzy we rush through the days and weeks, not living life, but consuming it.
— *Unknown*

INCH by inch, everything's a cinch.
— *Dr. Robert Schuller*

SMILE

THE world always looks better from behind a smile.   — *Anonymous*

ALL people smile in the same language. A smile is the talisman of friendship.   — *Anonymous*

WHAT sunshine is to flowers, smiles are to humanity.
                                                    — *Joseph Addison*

YOU CAN smile and smile and be a villain.   — *William Shakespeare*

SOLITUDE

I CAN enjoy society in a room; but out of doors, nature is company enough for me. I am then never less alone than when alone.
                                                    — *William Hazlitt*

CONVERSATION enriches the understanding; but solitude is the school of genius.   — *Edward Gibbon*

THE lives of great men reveal that each of them spent considerable time alone, away from the distractions where they had time to think. Solitude is a wise teacher.   — *Anonymous*

NO one can produce anything important unless he isolates himself.
                                                    — *Goethe*

HE who has tasted the sweetness of solitude and tranquility becomes free from fear and free from sin.   — *Buddha*

TO go into solitude, a man needs to retire as much from his chamber as from society ... If a man would be let alone, let him look at the stars.   — *Ralph Waldo Emerson*

I NEVER found the companion that was so companionable as solitude.   — *Henry David Thoreau*

EVERYONE has got to sit down and give their heart a chance to unfold and let the things that are deepest in you come up and speak to you.
— *Alfred A. Montapert*

SORROW

HAVE courage for the great sorrows of life, and patience for the small ones. And when you have accomplished your daily task, go to sleep in peace. God is awake.
— *Victor Hugo*

TO revive a forgotten sorrow is cruel.
— *Sophocles*

THERE is no sense in crying over spilt milk, why bewail what is done and cannot be recalled?
— *Sophocles*

BELIEVE me, every man has his secret sorrows which the world knows not; and oftentimes we call a man cold when he is only sad.
— *Henry Wadsworth Longfellow*

SOUL

THE soul is the seat of your being, the YOU of YOU. The Bible calls it "heart." It is the total invisible YOU ... THE TOTAL YOU IN THE SPIRIT.
— *Alfred A. Montapert*

THE soul, like the body, lives by what it feeds on.
— *Josiah G. Holland*

I AM fully convinced that the soul is indestructible, and that its activity will continue through eternity. It is like the sun, which, to our eyes, seems to set in night; but it has in reality only gone to diffuse its light elsewhere.
— *Goethe*

THE principal thing in this world is to keep one's soul aloft.
— *Gustave Flaubert*

SOUL

WE see the world piece by piece, as the sun, the moon, the animal, the tree; but the whole of which these are the shining parts, is the soul. — *Ralph Waldo Emerson*

IMMORTALITY will come to such as are fit for it; and he who would be a great soul in the future must be a great soul now.
— *Ralph Waldo Emerson*

I THINK that love is given us so that we can see a soul. And this soul we see is the highest conception of excellence and truth we can bring forth: This soul is our reflected self. And from seeing what one soul is, we imagine what all souls may be . . . and thus we reach God, who is the Universal Soul. — *Elbert G. Hubbard*

THE stars may fade away, the sun may grow dim with age, and nature sink in years, but the soul of man shall flourish in immortal youth, unhurt amid the war of the elements, the wreck of matter, and the crash of worlds. — *Joseph Addison*

THE soul is the aspect of ourselves that is specific of human nature. It distinguishes man from all other animals. We are not capable of defining this mysterious entity. It is hidden within the body, unnoticed by physiologists, pathologists, economists, and even ourselves; yet it is the most colossal power on this planet. Its invisible presence has transformed our universe. — *Alexis Carrel*

IT is the soul, and not the strong-box, that should be filled. — *Seneca*

CERTAIN thoughts are prayers . . . There are moments when, whatever the posture of the body, the Soul is on its knees. — *Victor Hugo*

GOD is the home of the soul, just as space is the home of the body.
— *Alfred A. Montapert*

FOR what shall it profit a man, if he gain the whole world, and lose his own soul? — *Mark 8:36*

SOW

YESTERDAY'S seeds are today's blossoms. We must recognize exactly what kind of seeds we are sowing today if we want to know what tomorrow's blossoms are going to be. — *Szekely*

YOU reap what you sow . . . not something else, but that. An act of love makes the soul loving. A deed of humbleness deepens humbleness. The thing reaped is the very thing sown, multiplied a hundred fold. You have sown a seed of life, you reap life everlasting.
— *F.W. Robertson*

WE sow a thought and reap an act. We sow an act and reap a habit. We sow a habit and reap a character. We sow a character and reap a destiny. — *William M. Thackeray*

SPACE

THERE is beauty in space, and it is orderly. There is no weather, and there is regularity. It is predictable . . . everything in space obeys the laws of physics. If you know these laws and obey them, space will treat you kindly. And don't tell me man doesn't belong there. Man belongs wherever he wants to go. — *Wernher Von Braun*

SPEECH

STAND up straight, Talk out boldly, And sit down quickly.
— *Martin Luther*

BY the word, one knows the workman. — *Jean de La Fontaine*

MEND your speech lest it mar your fortune. — *William Shakespeare*

DISCRETION of speech is more than eloquence; and to speak agreeably to him with whom we deal is more than to speak in good words or in good order. — *Sir Francis Bacon*

SPEECH

TALK is by far the most accessible of pleasures. It costs nothing in money, it is all profit, it completes our education, founds and fosters our friendships, and can be enjoyed at any age and in almost any state of health.
— *Robert Louis Stevenson*

SPEND

NO man is rich whose expenditures exceed his means! And no man is poor whose incomings exceed his outgoings.　— *Thomas C. Haliburton*

I ONLY ask that Fortune send
A little more than I shall spend.
— *Oliver Wendell Holmes*

SPIRIT

THUS, I assert that every good man, living or dead, is of spiritual nature and rightly called a Spirit.
— *Plato*

IT must be of the Spirit if we are to save the flesh.
— *Gen. Douglas MacArthur*

I BELIEVE that man will not merely endure, he will prevail. He is immortal, not because he alone among creatures has an inexhaustible voice, but because he has a soul, a spirit capable of compassion and sacrifice and endurance.
— *William Faulkner*

THERE are only two forces in the world . . . the sword and the spirit. In the long run the sword will always be conquered by the spirit.
— *Napoleon Bonaparte*

ONE truth stands firm. All that happens in world history rests on something spiritual. If the Spiritual is strong, it creates world history. If it is weak, it suffers world history.
— *Albert Schweitzer*

THE fruit of the Spirit is love, joy, peace, long-suffering, gentleness, goodness, faith, meekness, temperance. — *Galatians 5:22*

THE Divine Spirit within me always helps me to do better than I know how. — *Alfred A. Montapert*

SPIRITUAL

THE key to spiritual satisfaction is being right with God.
— *Billy Graham*

I HAVE a spiritual plant here that must be watered at least once a week. — *Ralph Waldo Emerson*

LIFE is sterile without the spiritual. — *Alfred A. Montapert*

WITH the years comes a certain ripening of the spirit. We come to see things as they are, and our mind becomes reconciled to the world as it is. Realization of the essential smallness, sordidness, and lack of completeness of the material life turns our mind to appreciation of the enduring satisfactions of the other and higher aspect of life, the spiritual life. — *Councillor*

SPIRITUAL DEVELOPMENT

GOD has placed in each soul an apostle to lead us upon the illumined path. Yet many seek life from without, unaware that it is within them. — *Kahlil Gibran*

SPIRITUAL development is a long and arduous journey, an adventure through strange lands full of surprises, joy, and beauty, difficulties and even dangers. — *Roberto Assagioli*

THE Sage follows not the eyes but the soul, not the senses but essence. — *Lao Tzu*

SPIRITUAL DEVELOPMENT

WE do not need more material development; we need more spiritual development; we do not need more law; we need more religion; we do not need more of the things that are seen; we need more of the things that are unseen. — *Calvin Coolidge*

MAN'S goal is to seek communion with the Presence behind the phenomena, and to seek it with the aim of bringing his self into harmony with this Absolute Reality. — *Arnold J. Toynbee*

YOU, and you alone, must assume responsibility for your own spiritual development. This must be accomplished by elevating your own consciousness through POSITIVE THINKING.
— *Walter M. Germain*

THE uprising of the spirit in the course of the evolution of every individual is more than a fundamental law of human life; it is its distinctive characteristic. — *Alexis Carrel*

OF all habits, the most harmful to spiritual progress are those of lying, intriguing, slandering and betraying one's neighbors, and of turning everything to one's own immediate advantage. The spirit can never develop in an atmosphere of corruption and falsehood.
— *Alexis Carrel*

THE kingdom of God within you is your growing ability to be all that you truly are. It is your power to be what you are created to be . . . the image or self-expression of the Infinite. — *J. Sig Paulson*

THE first thing to attend to is my SPIRITUAL DEVELOPMENT. This is the foundation stone of my life. With this I can cope with life and handle anything that comes my way. — *Alfred A. Montapert*

HE is blessed who is assured that the animal is dying out in him day by day, and the divine being established. — *Henry David Thoreau*

STARS

AMONG all the strange things that men have forgotten, the most universal and catastrophic lapse of memory is that by which they have forgotten they are living on a star. — *G.K. Chesterson*

ONLY that day dawns to which we are awake. There is more day to dawn. The sun is but a morning star. — *Henry David Thoreau*

STOCKS

STOCKS are the only game in town where you can decide to get out as you pour yourself a cup of coffee and be out by the time you have finished drinking it. This is called liquidity and it is worth an awful lot. — *William D. Montapert*

STRUGGLE

WE are not here to play, to dream, to drift; we have hard work to do and loads to lift; shun not the struggle . . . face it; 'tis God's gift. — *Lord Shaftsbury*

BEGIN thinking this very day of life as struggle rather than reward, and immediately you will feel that you are living as you were meant to live. — *John Miller*

THE important thing in the Olympic Games is not to win but to take part. The important thing in life is not the triumph but the struggle. The essential thing is not to have conquered but to have fought well. — *Pierre de Coubertin*

STUDY

STUDY gives strength to the mind; conversation, grace. — *Sir William Temple*

STUDY

SEIZE the moment of excited curiosity on any subject, to solve your doubts; for if you let it pass, the desire may never return, and you may remain in ignorance. — *William Wirt*

SUCCESS

SUCCESS is the achievement of happiness. — *William Benton*

SUCCESSFUL men usually snatch success from seeming failure. — *Anonymous*

SUCCESSFUL people make decisions quickly (as soon as all the facts are available) and change them very slowly (if ever). Unsuccessful people make decisions very slowly, and change them often and quickly. — *Napoleon Hill*

THERE is a close relationship between getting up in the world and getting up in the morning. — *Anonymous*

SUCCESS is not a "sometimes" thing. In other words, you don't do what is right once in a while, but all the time. Success is a habit. Winning is a habit. — *Vince Lombardi*

THERE is only one success ... to spend your life in your own way. —· *Christopher Morley*

THE secret of success is constancy of purpose. — *Benjamin Disraeli*

THREE qualities vital to success: TOIL, SOLITUDE, PRAYER. — *Carl Sandburg*

YOU don't "pay the price" for success, you ENJOY the price for success ... You pay the price for failure! — *Alfred A. Montapert*

TRUE Success depends ... More on Character than on Intellect. — *Alfred A. Montapert*

SUCCESS can be only one ingredient in happiness, and is too dearly purchased if all the other ingredients have been sacrificed to obtain it.   — *Bertrand Russell*

SUCCESS is not something that can be measured or worn on a watch or hung on the wall. It is not the esteem of colleagues, or the admiration of the community, or the appreciation of patients. Success is the certain knowledge that you have become yourself, the person you were meant to be from all time. That should be reward enough.
                                                                       — *Dr. George Sheehan*

IT is no use saying, "We are doing our best." You have got to succeed in doing what is necessary.   — *Sir Winston Churchill*

SUCCESS is discovering what God would have you do with your life.
                                                                       — *Mo Siegel*

THERE is no such thing as complete SUCCESS. An achievement is only a challenge to future progress. We never really arrive. We are always on the way.   — *Alfred A. Montapert*

INSTEAD Of thinking about where you are, think about where you want to be. It takes twenty hard working years to become an overnight success.   — *Diana Rankin*

SUCCESS is the old ABC'S . . . Ability, Breaks, and Courage.
                                                                       — *Charles Luckman*

I CANNOT give you the formula for success, but I can give you the formula for failure . . . which is: Try to please everybody.
                                                                       — *Herbert B. Swope*

THE common idea that success spoils people by making them vain, egotistic and self-complacent is erroneous; on the contrary, it makes them for the most part humble, tolerant, and kind. Failure makes people cruel and bitter.   — *W. Somerset Maugham*

SUCCESS

THE successful man is one who finds out what is the matter with his business before his competitors do. *— Roy L. Smith*

THE secret of living a successful life is not so much the culmination of great and grandiose projects, as it is learning to live well each day, and to measure oneself as the sun sets. *— Anonymous*

QUALIFICATIONS for SUCCESS: FIRST is a big wastebasket. You must know what to DISCARD. SECOND, it is as important to know what to PRESERVE. THIRD, do not offer nor accept unnecessary RESPONSIBILITIES. FOURTH, learn HOW and WHEN to say No. For developing the power to say NO gives us the capacity to say YES. *— The Way To Happiness*

ONE great, I might almost say the greatest, element of success and happiness in life is the capacity for honest, solid work. *— John Lubbock*

SIX word formula for success: Think things through . . . then follow through. *— Eddie Rickenbacker*

SUFFERING

PRAY that suffering and sorrow may serve to purify and strengthen you. *— James Keller*

NOTHING happens to any man which he is not formed by nature to bear. *— Marcus Aurelius*

OUT of suffering have emerged the strongest souls. *— Edwin H. Chapin*

THERE is only one road to true human greatness . . . the road through suffering. *— Albert Einstein*

SUFFERING does not produce growth directly; suffering is growing the hard way. *— Alfred A. Montapert*

SUNSHINE

SUNRISE is often lovelier than noon.   *— Thomas Carlyle*

THOSE who bring sunshine into the lives of others cannot keep it from themselves.   *— J.M. Barrie*

THE sun brings out the best in us.
— Alfred A. Montapert

ALL sunshine makes the desert.   *— Arab Proverb*

SUNSHINE is delicious, rain is refreshing, wind braces up, snow is exhilarating. There is really no such thing as bad weather, only different kinds of good weather.

— John Ruskin

SURVIVAL

EVERY living thing wishes to survive. Just as the plant seeks the light, just as the earth is fruitful, so there are instincts to survive, grow, unfold and fulfill.   *— Alfred A. Montapert*

WHEN you play cat and mouse, always be the cat.   *— Anonymous*

TACT

TALENT is power, tact is skill. Talent knows what to do; tact knows how to do it.   *— Anonymous*

WITHOUT tact you can learn nothing. Tact teaches you when to be silent. Inquirers who are always inquiring never learn anything.
— Benjamin Disraeli

TACT consists in knowing how far we may go too far.

— Jean Cocteau

TACT

TACT comes as much from goodness of heart as from fineness of taste.
— *Endymion*

TACT is the knack of making a point without making an enemy.
— *Howard W. Newton*

MORE unhappiness is caused by want of thought, or of tact, than by want of heart.
— *John Lubbock*

TALENT

THE real tragedy of life is not in being limited to one talent, but in the failure to use the one talent.
— *Edgar Work*

HIDE not your talents, they for use were made. What's a sundial in the Shade?
— *Benjamin Franklin*

TALK

AS a man grows wiser he talks less and says more.
— *Roger Babson*

MANY people talk, not because they have anything to say, but for the mere love of talking. Talking should be an exercise of the brain, rather than the tongue.
— *John Lubbock*

IN the company of strangers silence is safe.
— *Anonymous*

TASK

DO thine own task, and be therewith content.
— *Goethe*

THERE is no magic by which to accomplish a difficult task. "By the sweat of thy brow" is the only road to success.
— *Alfred A. Montapert*

A TASK! To be honest, to be kind; to earn a little and to spend a little less; to make upon the whole a family happier for his presence; to renounce when that shall be necessary, and not to be embittered; to keep a few friends, but these without capitulation; above all, on the same grim condition, to keep friends with himself, here is a task for all that man has of fortitude and delicacy.

— *Robert Louis Stevenson*

THE man who has not learned the secret of taking the drudgery out of his task by flinging his whole soul into it, has not learned the first principles of success or happiness. — *O.S. Marden*

TASTE

GOOD taste is the flower of good sense. — *Achille Poincelot*

TO have taste, one must have some soul. — *Vauvenargues*

GOOD taste comes more from judgment than from the mind.

— *La Rochefoucauld*

TAXES

IF you don't take your tax deductions, you will never get them.

— *Alfred A. Montapert*

I PLACE economy among the first and most important virtues, and public debt as the greatest of dangers to be feared. To preserve our independence, we must not let our rulers load us with perpetual debt. If we run into such debts, we must be taxed in our meat and drink, in our necessities and in our comforts, in our labor and in our amusements. If we can prevent the government from wasting the labor of the people, under the pretense of caring for them, they will be happy. — *Thomas Jefferson*

TAXES

THE art of taxation consists in so plucking the goose as to obtain the largest possible amount of feathers with the smallest possible amount of hissing.
— *Jean B. Colbert*

TEACHING

YOU teach best what you most need to learn.
— *Richard Bach*

THE best teacher is . . . the one who kindles an inner fire, arouses moral enthusiasm, inspires the student with a vision of what he may become, and reveals the worth and permanency of moral and cultural and spiritual values.
— *Harold Garnett*

TEACH me Thy way, O Lord, and lead me in a plain path.
— *Psalm 27:11*

COME forth into the light of things, let Nature be your teacher.
— *William Wordsworth*

TEARS

TEARS are the safety valve of the heart.
— *Anonymous*

TECHNOLOGY

OURS is a world of nuclear giants and ethical infants. If we continue to develop our technology without wisdom or prudence, our servant may prove to be our executioner.
— *Gen. Omar Bradley*

TEMPER

REMEMBER that when you're in the right you can afford to keep your temper, and when you're in the wrong you can't afford to lose it.
— *Mahatma Gandhi*

A LITTLE pot boils easily. — *Dutch Proverb*

WHEN a man's temper gets the best of him . . . it reveals the worst of him. — *Anonymous*

OUR temperaments differ in capacity of heat, or we boil at different degrees. — *Ralph Waldo Emerson*

TEMPTATION

MAN'S chief merit consists in resisting the impulses of his nature. — *Samuel Johnson*

NEVER do anything of which you will have cause to be ashamed. — *John Lubbock*

'TIS one thing to be tempted, another thing to fall. — *William Shakespeare*

A MAN is no stronger than his weakest moment, and every man has his Achilles heel, a point of vulnerability. We cannot escape temptation because we are endowed with freedom of choice. And since no person has an iron will, everyone is in danger of falling. We can choose between good and evil, true and false, between being generous and selfish, between being brave and cowardly. And the very freedom of choice becomes in itself temptation. — *Charles Allen*

BETTER shun the bait than struggle in the snare. — *John Dryden*

TENSION

TENSION is the mortal enemy of energy. — *Anonymous*

THE surgeon can cut out the ulcer, but he can't cut out the tensions. — *Dr. Walter Alvarez*

IF anything bugs you, get rid of it. — *Alfred A. Montapert*

TESTIMONY

IT is the business of the Christian church to carry the testimony of the Gospel of Jesus Christ. The first business of the church is not preaching. Our first business is to carry His message by word of testimony. For there is nothing so thrilling, nothing so gripping, nothing so fascinating as the word of an individual who has experienced the Grace of God.   — *Alfred A. Montapert*

THEOLOGY

THEOLOGY deserves to be called the highest wisdom, for everything is viewed in the light of the first cause.   — *St. Thomas Aquinas*

THINK

THEY CAN ... because they ... THINK they CAN.   — *Virgil*

WISE men think without talking. Fools talk without thinking.
          — *Anonymous*

THINKING is the talking of the soul with itself.   — *Plato*

VERY little is needed to make a happy life. It is ALL within yourself ... in your WAY of thinking!   — *Marcus Aurelius*

FEW people think more than two or three times a year ... I have made an international reputation for myself by thinking once or twice a week.   — *George Bernard Shaw*

AVOID DESTRUCTIVE THINKING. Improper negative thoughts sink people. A ship can sail on water all around the world many, many times, but just let enough water get into the ship and it will sink. Just so with the human mind. Let enough negative thoughts or improper thoughts get into the human mind and the person sinks just like the ship.   — *Alfred A. Montapert*

READING furnishes the mind only with materials of knowledge; it is thinking that makes what we read ours. — *John Locke*

STRAIGHT thinking starts with facts. Careless thinking starts with opinions. — *William J. Reilly*

THOUGHT

THE finest piece of sculpture which Michelangelo ever carved began with a thought. — *Anonymous*

A THOUGHT is mental dynamite. — *Elbert G. Hubbard*

OUR positive thoughts of today will be the realities of tomorrow. — *Dr. Paul Parker*

GREAT thoughts reduced to practice become great acts. — *William Hazlitt*

A MAN would do well to carry a pencil in his pocket and write down the thoughts of the moment. Those that come unsought for are commonly the most valuable and should be secured, because they seldom return. — *Sir Francis Bacon*

THOUGHT is the seed of action. — *Ralph Waldo Emerson*

EACH of us must live off the fruit of our thoughts. — *Anonymous*

NOTHING is more important to YOU than this: YOU . . . are the sole master of your Thought Process! "As a man THINKETH in his HEART so is he." This is a Law as real as the Law of Gravity. — *Alfred A. Montapert*

WE magnetize into our lives whatever we hold in our thought. — *Richard Bach*

ALL that we are is the result of what we have thought. — *Buddha*

THOUGHT

CHANGE your thoughts and you change your world.

— *Norman Vincent Peale*

YOU are today where your thoughts have brought you; you will be tomorrow where your thoughts take you. — *James Allen*

ALL truly wise thoughts have been thought already thousands of times; but to make them truly ours, we must think them over again honestly, till they take root in our personal experience. — *Goethe*

THE world in which we live is determined by our thoughts.

— *Marcus Aurelius*

WHATSOEVER things are true, whatsoever things are honest, whatsoever things are just, whatsoever things are pure, whatsoever things are lovely, whatsoever things are of good report; if there be any virtue, and if there be any praise, think on these things.

— *Philippians 4:8*

THRIFT

THRIFT is care and good judgment in the spending of one's means.

— *Unknown*

TIME

TIME is the sure test for Everything. — *Alfred A. Montapert*

TIME is but the stream I go a-fishing in. I drink at it; but while I drink I see the sandy bottom and detect how shallow it is. Its thin current slides away, but eternity remains. — *Henry David Thoreau*

SO much of our time is preparation, so much is routine, and so much retrospect, that the path of each man's genius contracts itself to a very few hours. — *Ralph Waldo Emerson*

TIME

LIFE is but a moment, death also is but another.
— *Dr. Robert Schuller*

EVALUATE how you spend your time; eliminate some activities to give you more time to achieve your goals; organize activities so you spend more time with the most productive ones, and review your efforts carefully. — *Alfred A. Montapert*

GATHER ye rosebuds while ye may,
Old Time is still a-flying;
And this same flower that smiles today,
Tomorrow will be dying. — *Robert Herrick*

THE important question is not how many days or years we have lived, but how much we have thought and felt. — *Alexis Carrel*

SO TEACH us to number our days, that we may apply our hearts unto wisdom. — *Psalm 90:12*

WASTE your own time if you must, but not the time of others. Time is valuable to some. — *Alfred A. Montapert*

YOU'LL never find time for anything . . . if you want it, you'll have to make it. — *Anonymous*

IF, before going to bed every night, you will tear a page from the calendar, and remark, "There goes another day of my life, never to return," you will soon become time conscious. — *A.B. Zu Tavern*

TO live successfully one must have a definite plan and be aware that there is a limited time in which to get the job done. Most of us fail because we aim at nothing in particular and keep hitting the mark . . . then when time is almost run out we frantically try to "make up for lost time," but "lost time" cannot be recovered. — *Alfred A. Montapert*

TIME

TO everything there is a season, and a time to every purpose under heaven: A time to be born, and a time to die; a time to plant, and a time to pluck up that which is planted; A time to kill, and a time to heal; a time to break down, and a time to build up; A time to weep, and a time to laugh; a time to mourn, and a time to dance; A time to cast away stones, and a time to gather stones together; a time to embrace, and a time to refrain from embracing; A time to get, and a time to lose; a time to keep, and a time to cast away; A time to rend, and a time to sew; a time to keep silence, and a time to speak; A time to love, and a time to hate; a time of war, and a time of peace.

— Ecclesiastes III, 1-8

TIME is not measured by the passing of years, but by what one does, what one feels, and what one achieves.   *— Jawaharlal Nehru*

EVERY man will gravitate to his own level, just give him time.

— Anonymous

TIME MANAGEMENT/USE/WASTE

WE shall never have more time. We have, and have always had, all the time there is. No object is served in waiting until next week or even until tomorrow. Keep going day in and out. Concentrate on something useful. Having decided to achieve a task, achieve it at all costs.   *— Arnold Bennett*

YOU have to live on this twenty-four hours of daily time. Out of it you have to spin health, pleasure, money, content, respect, and the evolution of your immortal soul. Its right use, its most effective use, is a matter of the highest urgency and of the most thrilling actuality.

— Arnold Bennett

DOST thou love life? Then do not squander time, for that is the stuff life is made of.   *— Benjamin Franklin*

THE man who can master his time can master nearly everything.
— *Bernard Baruch*

THINK in the morning, act in the noon, eat in the evening, sleep in the night.
— *William Blake*

HE who every morning plans the transactions of the day, and follows out that plan, carries a thread that will guide him through the labyrinth of the most busy life. The orderly arrangement of his time is like a ray of light that darts itself through all his occupations. But where no plan is laid, where the disposal of time is surrendered merely to the chance of accident, chaos will soon reign.
— *Victor Hugo*

TIME is what we want most, but what, alas! we use worst.
— *William Penn*

A WISE man does not spend his time, he invests it.
— *Alfred A. Montapert*

IF you don't have time to do it right . . . you may have to find time to do it over.
— *Anonymous*

THE more a man has to do, the more he is able to accomplish, for he learns to economize his time.
— *Sir Matthew Hale*

IT takes less time to do a thing right, than it does to explain why you did it wrong.
— *Henry Wadsworth Longfellow*

LOST, yesterday, somewhere between sunrise and sunset, two golden hours, each set with sixty diamond minutes. No reward is offered, for they are gone forever.
— *Horace Mann*

MANY people take no care of their money till they come nearly to the end of it, and others do just the same with their time.
— *Goethe*

TIME MANAGEMENT/USE/WASTE

ACCOMPLISHMENTS will soar and mount
If wasted time is made to count.   *— Ruth Lommatzsch*

THE man who wastes today lamenting yesterday will waste tomorrow
lamenting today.   *— Philip M. Raskin*

TIMING

A MAN must wait for the right moment.   *— Schopenhauer*

TO be right too soon is the equivalent of being wrong. Things usually
take longer to happen than is generally supposed. TIMING IS THE
MASTER KEY TO MAKING MONEY.   *— William D. Montapert*

I OWE everything in the world to being always a quarter of an hour
beforehand.   *— Lord Horatio Nelson*

TODAY

THE man who does his best today will be a hard man to beat
tomorrow.   *— Anonymous*

YESTERDAY is a cancelled check; tomorrow is a promissory note.
Today is ready cash . . . spend it wisely.   *— Anonymous*

NO matter how old you are you have never lived THIS day. This day
is a new piece of road. Better ask GOD for directions.
          — Alfred A. Montapert

THIS is the day which the Lord hath made; We will rejoice and be
glad in it.   *— Psalm 118:24*

THE best time to do anything is right between yesterday and
tomorrow.   *— Anonymous*

WRITE it in your heart that every day is the best day of your year.
          — Ralph Waldo Emerson

IN the morning fix thy good purpose; and at night examine thyself what thou hast done, how thou hast behaved thyself in word, deed and thought.
— Thomas a Kempis

YESTERDAY is but today's memory, and tomorrow is today's dream.
— Kahlil Gibran

THE seeds you plant today, you will harvest in due season. As ye sow, so shall ye reap.
— Alfred A. Montapert

TOIL

WHAT I have done is due to past thought.
— Sir Isaac Newton

THE highest reward for man's toil is not what he gets for it, but what he becomes by it.
— John Ruskin

THE busier we are, the more acutely we feel that we live.
— Immanuel Kant

DO what you can, with what you have, where you are.
— Theodore Roosevelt

TOLERANCE

IF you wish men to bear with you, you must bear with them.
— Anonymous

TOMORROW

TOMORROW is a new day; you shall begin it well and serenely and with too high a spirit to be encumbered with your old nonsense.
— Ralph Waldo Emerson

I AM not afraid of tomorrow, for I have seen yesterday and I love today.
— William A. White

TONGUE

IF thou desire to be wise, be so wise as to hold thy tongue.

— Anonymous

WATCH thy tongue; out of it are the issues of life. *— Thomas Carlyle*

TRAGEDY

DOING the lower when the higher is possible constitutes one of the greatest tragedies in a man's life. *— O.S. Marden*

THE tragedy of life is not so much what men suffer but rather what they miss. *— Thomas Carlyle*

THERE is only one thing to do when confronted by tragedy of any kind, caused by circumstances beyond human control . . . and that's to start rebuilding and remaking one's life as best one can. This, in any unforeseen adversity, I resolve to do. *— Harold Sherman*

THERE are NO tragedies . . . just FACTS NOT RECOGNIZED IN TIME. *— William D. Montapert*

TRAVEL

ALL travel has its advantages. If the traveller visits better countries, he may learn to improve his own; and if fortune carries him to worse, he may learn to enjoy his own. *— Samuel Johnson*

THE fool wanders, the wise man travels. *— Thomas Fuller*

TRAVEL for the young is a part of education, and for the elder is a part of experience. *— Sir Francis Bacon*

I AM a part of all that I have seen. *— Alfred Lord Tennyson*

THE world belongs to those who have seen it. *— Anonymous*

THE advantages of travel last through life; and often as we sit at home some bright and perfect view of Venice, of Paris, London, Florence, or Rome comes back to us with pleasant memories of days wisely spent in travel.
— *Alfred A. Montapert*

TRIALS

GOD does not take away trials or carry us over them but strengthens us through them.
— *Henry Wadsworth Longfellow*

THERE are THREE ways that prepare us for life's trials: One is the Spartan way that says, "I have strength within me to do it. I am captain of my soul. With the courage and will that is mine I will be master when the struggle comes." The second way is in the spirit of Socrates, who affirmed that we have minds, reason and judgment to evaluate and help us cope with the enigmas and struggles of life. The third approach is the Christian way. It does not exclude the first two, but it adds, "You begin with God, who is the Higher Power. When your strength grows weak and your reason fails you, FAITH in the Creator gives you THE POWER to overcome all things."
— *Alfred A. Montapert*

THE diamond cannot be polished without friction, nor the man perfected without trials.
— *Anonymous*

IT is by presence of mind in untried emergencies that the native metal of man is tested.
— *James R. Lowell*

LET the stones in your pathway be stepping stones to success.
— *Anonymous*

TRIFLES

IT is the mark of a great man to treat trifles as trifles, and important matters as important.
— *Gotthold E. Lessing*

TRIFLES

THEY that employ their minds too much upon trifles commonly make themselves incapable of anything that is serious or great.
— *La Rochefoucauld*

THUS, the smallest circumstances may determine destruction. As trains are destroyed by the movement of a switch no more than the tenth part of an inch, so trifles sometimes determine, in a critical hour, men's fate for time and eternity. — *H. F. Kletzing*

DON'T fuss about trifles. Don't permit little things ... the mere termites of life ... to ruin your happiness. — *Dale Carnegie*

TRIUMPH

YOUTH is the time for the adventures of the body ... but age for the triumph of the mind. — *Logan Pearsall Smith*

TROUBLE

WE don't deliberately look for trouble in life. It comes. Suffering is a Universal fact ... no one can escape its claws. The rain falls on the just and the unjust. We all face personal Armageddons.
— *Billy Graham*

IF you want to live without trouble, you'll have to die young. For if one thing is sure, it's that trouble has always been with us and always will be. — *Oliver Wendell Holmes*

THE less we talk about our troubles, the sooner they will disappear.
— *A.P. Gouthey*

IN the world ye shall have tribulation. — *John 16:33*

ANYONE can hold the helm when the sea is calm. — *Publilius Syrus*

WHEN a man has a small trouble, he can laugh it off, but when he has a big trouble . . . a real trouble . . . he should go for a long walk. He should walk at least five miles quickly. That will take the blood out of his head. It will help to put him in control of himself.

— *George M. Cohan*

DON'T invite trouble . . . it always accepts. — *Alfred A. Montapert*

TRUST/DISTRUST

TRUST thyself: Every heart vibrates to that iron string.

— *Ralph Waldo Emerson*

HE that takes truth for his guide, and duty for his end, may safely trust to God's providence to lead him aright. — *Blaise Pascal*

ALWAYS to distrust is an error, as well as always to trust. — *Goethe*

DISTRUST all in whom the impulse to lead is powerful.

— *Frederick Nietzsche*

TRUTH

I HAVE searched for TRUTH early and late. TRUTH is all I will have when I come to the end of my little day. — *Alfred A. Montapert*

MEN occasionally stumble on the truth, but most of them pick themselves up and hurry off as if nothing had happened.

— *Sir Winston Churchill*

IN accumulating property for ourselves or our posterity, in founding a family or a state, or acquiring fame, even we are mortal; but in dealing with truth we are immortal, and need fear no change nor accident. — *Henry David Thoreau*

TRUTH

THIS above all ... to thine own self be true; And it must follow, as the night the day, Thou canst not then be false to any man.
— *William Shakespeare*

AND ye shall know the truth, and the truth shall make you free.
— *John 8:32*

THE truth is not always the same as the majority opinion.
— *Pope Jean Paul*

TO be known as an honest, earnest seeker after truth is to rank high in God's estimation. Few things rank above it.   — *Alfred A. Montapert*

I AM the way, the truth, and the life; no man cometh unto the Father but by me.   — *John 14:6*

MEASURED objectively, what a man can wrest from Truth by passionate striving is utterly infinitesimal. But the striving frees us from the bonds of the self and makes us comrades of those who are the best and the greatest.   — *Albert Einstein*

GO not abroad; retire into yourself, for truth dwells in the inner man.   — *St. Augustine*

THE heart of him that hath understanding seeketh knowledge: but the mouth of fools feedeth on foolishness.   — *Proverbs 15:14*

I WOULD gladly give my life if it would advance the cause of truth.
— *Alexander Solzhenitsyn*

GOD made Truth with many doors to welcome every believer who knocks on them.   — *John Stuart Mill*

TO speak the truth is good ... to Know the truth is better ... but to live and experience the truth is truly ennobling. — *Alfred A. Montapert*

ALL modes of truth are in God.   — *Pietro Pompanazzi*

FAITH perceives Truth sooner than Experience can.   — *Kahlil Gibran*

SAY not, I have found the truth, but rather, I have found a truth.
                                                   — *Kahlil Gibran*

IN learning to follow the light of our own spirituality, we find our
awareness of Truth increasing day by day.   — *Leddy Schmelig*

BUY the truth and sell it not.   — *Anonymous*

SOMETHING inside of me is searching for the truth which feeds the
greatest of all hunger, which is the hunger to strengthen our
relationship with God.   — *Alfred A. Montapert*

TRY

WE know now that most people can do almost anything with
reasonable success if they are willing to try with the best that is in
them. We have not yet discovered the way to make most of us want
to try. Psychology may some day solve the problem. But why wait,
when we see that those who do try are the successful, happy ones.
                                                   — *William Ross*

NOTHING is hard if you try.   — *Anonymous*

MOST of the important things in the world have been accomplished
by people who have kept on trying when there seemed to be no hope
at all.   — *Dale Carnegie*

UNDERSTAND

THOSE who have the largest hearts have the soundest understand-
ings; and he is the truest philosopher who can forget himself.
                                                   — *William Hazlitt*

UNDERSTAND

TO get people to understand our point of view, we must first try to understand theirs. — *Sidney Keyes*

MOST of the important things that human beings ought to understand cannot be comprehended in youth. — *Robert M. Hutchins*

I HAVE made a ceaseless effort not to ridicule, not to bewail, not to scorn human actions, but to understand them. — *Baruch Spinoza*

UNHAPPY

WE degrade life by our follies and vices, and then complain that the unhappiness which is only their accompaniment is inherent in the constitution of things. — *Christian N. Bovee*

IF any man be unhappy, let him remember that he is unhappy by reason of himself alone. — *Epictetus*

UNIVERSE

LET man's first study be the knowledge of the Nature of the Universe. — *Lucretius*

GOD, the Great Giver, can open the whole universe to our gaze in the narrow space of a single line. — *Rabindranath Tagore*

USE

THE more a muscle works, the more it develops. Instead of wearing out, it is strengthened by activity. On the contrary, it atrophies if not used. The law of effort must be obeyed by brain and glands, as well as by muscles. — *Alexis Carrel*

USE

THIS is the true joy of life, the being used for a purpose recognized by yourself as a mighty one; the being thoroughly worn out before you are thrown on the scrap heap; the being a force of nature instead of a feverish little clod of ailments and grievances complaining that the world will not devote itself to making you happy
— George Bernard Shaw

FEW minds wear out, more rust out. *— Christian N. Bovee*

WHAT is the use of health or of life, if not to do some work therewith? *— Thomas Carlyle*

IT is one thing to know a lot, another thing to use it. *— Anonymous*

LET your daily wisdom of life be in making a good use of the opportunities given you. *— William Blackie*

A USELESS life is an early death. *— Goethe*

VALUES

MAN'S value is in the few things he creates and not in the many possessions he amasses. *— Kahlil Gibran*

WHAT we obtain too cheap we esteem too little; it is dearness only that gives everything its value. *— Thomas Paine*

I WONDER if the day will ever come when a full heart and a full head will count as much as a full purse. *— Alfred A. Montapert*

TOO many men who know all about financial values know nothing about human values. *— Roy L. Smith*

VALUES

MONEY isn't the most important thing to save. It is the least. Better to save your self-respect, your honor, your individual independence, your pride in being, and your health. These, and many more, are far better than gold. And their dividends are never passed.

— George Adams

HAPPINESS and contentment are not commodities which we import; neither do they depend upon "the abundance of things" which we possess. It is not where we are, what we have, or what we possess that makes us happy or unhappy. It is WHAT WE ARE that determines our state. *— Alfred A. Montapert*

A WISE man should have money in his head but not in his heart.

— Sir Francis Bacon

WE know the worth of a thing when we have lost it.

— French Proverb

TODAY we are afraid of simple words like GOODNESS and MERCY and KINDNESS. We don't believe in the good old words because we don't believe in the good old values anymore. And that's why the world is sick. *— Lin Yutang*

IF a nation values anything more than freedom, it will lose its freedom; and the irony of it is that if it is comfort or money it values more, it will lose that too. *— W. Somerset Maugham*

WHAT we seek is amusement, rather than spiritual uplift, achievement, love, peace, the great ideas men have always fought for. We are settling for games and toys. Our values are like the merchandise we buy: convenient, lightweight, disposable. They don't make frying pans like they use to . . . nor values. *— Sam Levenson*

VANITY

LET not him that is deceived trust in vanity; for vanity shall be his recompence. *— Job 15:31*

WHEN a man is wrapped up in himself . . . he makes a pretty small package.
— *Anonymous*

VICE

THE chief vice of many people consists not in doing evil, but in permitting it.
— *Roy Pearson*

WHEN a young man begins to go down hill everything seems to be greased for the occasion.
— *Josh Billings*

VICES are learned without a master.
— *Thomas Fuller*

IT has been my experience that folks who have no vices have very few virtues.
— *Abraham Lincoln*

SOME young men have an idea that there is something "manly" in vice. But any weak fool can be vicious. To be virtuous you must be a man; to be virtuous is to be truly free; vice is the real slavery.
— *John Lubbock*

VICTORY

WHEN you see a man living victoriously, do not assume that it is because his life is easier than another's. More likely it is because he has been more triumphant in his struggle.
— *John Miller*

WITH GOD'S WORD in your heart . . . each day is a VICTORIOUS DAY.
— *Evelyn W. Montapert*

YOU cannot win a VICTORY without a BATTLE.
— *Alfred A. Montapert*

VIRTUE

THE strength of a man's virtue is not to be measured by the efforts he makes under pressure, but by his ordinary conduct. — *Blaise Pascal*

VIRTUE

DEVELOP such virtues as patience, kindness, justice, love, unselfishness, tolerance, peace, and joy. With our minds fully occupied with these things, there will be no room for others.   — *William Ross*

HOME is the chief school of human virtue.   — *W.E. Channing*

IT is as foolish not to be virtuous as to put water instead of oil into an internal combustion engine.   — *Alexis Carrel*

VIRTUE ... is an act of the will, a habit which increases the quantity, intensity, and quality of life.   — *Alexis Carrel*

ASSUME a virtue if you have it not.   — *William Shakespeare*

TO be able everywhere one goes to carry five things into practice constitutes virtue. They are courtesy, magnanimity, sincerity, earnestness, and kindness. With courtesy you avoid insult. With magnanimity you win all. With sincerity men will trust you. With earnestness you will have success. With kindness you will be fit to command others.   — *Confucius*

VISION

HE who cherishes a beautiful vision, a lofty ideal in his heart, will one day realize it. Dream lofty dreams, and as you dream, so shall you become.   — *James Allen*

IF you have built castles in the air, your work need not be lost; that is where they should be. Now put the foundations under them.
    — *Henry David Thoreau*

HUNDREDS can talk to one who can think; thousands can think to one who can perceive.   — *John Ruskin*

IF I seem to see more than other men, it is because I stand on the shoulders of others. — *Albert Einstein*

VISUALIZE what you want to achieve. Every time you throw home a mental suggestion you are giving the subconscious mind a blueprint to go by. — *Henry Miller*

VITAMIN 'C'

VITAMIN C is one of the most important of our foods. People who take the optimum amount of vitamin C may well have, at each age, only one quarter as much illness and chance of dying as those who do not take extra vitamin C. This way of improving one's health will not, I believe, be ignored much longer. As people get older, they need more of this vitamin and also other vitamins to keep in good health.
— *Dr. Linus Pauling*

WAGE

I WORKED for a menial's hire.
Only to learn, dismayed,
That any wage I had asked of Life,
Life would have paid. — *Jessie B. Rittenhouse*

WAIT

EVERYTHING comes to him who hustles while he waits.
— *Thomas Alva Edison*

TO know how to wait is the great secret of success.
— *Joseph De Maistre*

I WOULD learn to wait for the best and have the wisdom to know when it comes. — *A. P. Gouthey*

ALL good abides with him who waiteth wisely.
— *Henry David Thoreau*

WALK

WALKING is one of the best forms of exercise. It confers physical, mental, and spiritual benefits. Right walking puts a tingle in the blood, promotes digestion, clarifies the mind, and elevates the spirit.
— *Grenville Kleiser*

THE best medicine: Two miles of oxygen a day. This is not only the best, but cheap and pleasant to take. It suits all ages and constitutions. It is patented by infinite wisdom, sealed with a signet divine . . . This medicine never fails. Spurious compounds are found in large towns; but get into the country lanes, among green field, or on the mountain top, and you have it in perfection as prepared in the great laboratory of nature.
— *Dr. Hinsdale*

WANTS

IT is not good to be too free. It is not good to have everything one wants.
— *Blaise Pascal*

THERE are two things to aim at in life: first, to get what you want; and after that to enjoy it. Only the wisest of mankind achieve the second.
— *Logan Pearsall Smith*

HALF the confusion in the world comes from not knowing how little we need. Riches are not from abundance of worldly goods but from a contented mind.
— *Anonymous*

WAR

THERE will one day spring from the brain of Science a machine of force so fearful in its potentialities, so absolutely terrifying, that even man, the fighter who will dare torture and death in order to inflict torture and death, will be appalled, and so will abandon war forever.
— *Thomas Alva Edison*

WAR is the business of barbarians.
— *Napoleon Bonaparte*

THE West has erred because it has chosen to fight Communism with Communism's own material weapons. As long as the battle is fought on these terms, the Communists will keep on winning. The West must base its appeal on more than freedom, more than prosperity; it must base its appeal on religion. Only in this way can democracy turn the tables on the Communist assailants. The grace of God might bring about this miracle. — *Arnold Toynbee*

WASTE

WASTE is worse than loss. The time is coming when every person who lays claim to ability will keep the question of waste before him constantly. The scope of thrift is limitless. — *Thomas Alva Edison*

WASTE not, want not, willful waste makes woeful want. — *St. Basil*

SHORT as life is, we make it still shorter by the careless waste of time. — *Victor Hugo*

EVERYONE should keep a big mental wastepaper basket, and the older he grows, the more things he will promptly consign to it. — *Samuel Butler*

THE greatest waste is the waste of a positive idea that comes from God! — *Robert Schuller*

THINK that day lost whose low descending sun,
Views from thy hand no noble action done. — *Jacob Bobart*

TO make the most of ourselves, we must cut off whatever drains vitality . . . physical or moral . . . and stop all the waste of life. — *Alfred A. Montapert*

WEAK

THE weak are never strengthened by weakening the strong. — *Anonymous*

WEALTH

THOSE who are rich in faith are the only really wealthy.

— *Anonymous*

IT is not in everyone's power to secure wealth, office, or honors; but everyone may be good, generous, and wise. — *Vauvenargues*

CHILDREN are a poor man's wealth. — *Danish Proverb*

I FIND, where I thought myself poor, there was I most rich.

— *Ralph Waldo Emerson*

HE is richest who is content with the least, for content is the wealth of nature. — *Socrates*

WHAT wealth it is to have such friends that we cannot think of them without elevation. — *Henry David Thoreau*

YOUR real wealth is what you are inside, Not what you OWN or HAVE . . . Possessions are outside of you, Treasures are inside of you.

— *Alfred A. Montapert*

THE real wealth of a man is not the amount of his bank account. Money weighs as light as down against the gold of CHARACTER.

— *Alfred A. Montapert*

WICKED

A WICKED life leads to a wicked death. — *Moliere*

WIFE

TEACHER, tender comrade, wife,
A fellow companion through life. — *Robert Louis Stevenson*

HEAVEN will be no heaven to me if I do not meet my wife there.

— *Andrew Jackson*

FREE WILL

YOU'RE always free to change your mind and choose a different future.
— *Richard Bach*

EACH of us is capable today, at this moment, of discovering a whole new way of life.
— *Leddy Schmelig*

WE are not able to do all that we please. In some directions we can develop ourselves; in other directions we are stopped by a barrier . . . Of our own free will we have to remain within the natural law of our being. Nothing succeeds in the long run unless it conforms itself to the law of nature and to the will of God.
— *Alexis Carrel*

LAST WILL

I HAVE now disposed of all my property to my family. There is one thing more I wish I could give them and that is the Christian religion. If they had this and I had not given them one shilling, they would be rich, and if they had not that and I had given them all the world they would be poor.
— *Patrick Henry*

A WILL of your own is more likely to help you succeed than the will of a rich relative.
— *Anonymous*

WILL POWER

WHAT you wish to be, that you are, for such is the force of our will, joined to the Supreme, that whatever we wish to be, seriously, and with a true intention, that we become.
— *Jean Paul Richter*

PEOPLE do not lack strength; they lack will.
— *Victor Hugo*

NOTHING is impossible to the man who can will, and then do; this is the only law of success.
— *Mirabeau*

WILL POWER

THE difference between a successful person and others is not a lack of strength, not a lack of knowledge, but rather in a lack of will.

— Vince Lombardi

THE education of the will is the object of our existence . . . a character is a completely finished will. *— J. S. Hill*

WIN/WINNER

YOU can't win any games unless you are ready to win.

— Connie Mack

IT is not genius that wins, but hard work and a pure life.

— Elihu Burritt

A MAN can win anything if he puts his all in it. *— Anonymous*

YOU can't win today's game with the points you made yesterday.

— Alfred A. Montapert

GIVE me a man with common sense and good judgment . . . and I will give you a winner! *— Dick Roosevelt*

FOCUS on your future. Losers look backward, winners look forward. Discuss your hopes, dreams, plans . . . the steps you are taking to insure continual progress toward new and higher goals.

— Dr. William Appleton

WISDOM

LIFE'S tragedy is that we get old too soon and wise too late.

— Benjamin Franklin

TRUE wisdom is to know what is best worth knowing, and to do what is best worth doing. *— Hubert Humphrey*

WISDOM is the right use of knowledge.   — *Charles Q. Spurgeon*

MAKE wisdom your provision for the journey from youth to old age for it is a more certain support than all other possessions. — *Diogenes*

WISDOM is to the soul what health is to the body.
                                                 — *La Rochefoucauld*

TO be patient in little things, to be tolerant in large affairs and in the faults of others, to be happy in the midst of cares and problems . . . that is WISDOM.   — *Evelyn W. Montapert*

LIFE is the gift of Nature . . . but beautiful living is the gift of wisdom.   — *Greek Adage*

THE mintage of wisdom is to know that rest is rust, and that real life is in love, laughter, and work.   — *Elbert G. Hubbard*

TO finish the moment, to find the journey's end in every step of the road, to live the greatest number of good hours, is wisdom.
                                              — *Ralph Waldo Emerson*

THE most evident sign of wisdom is continued cheerfulness.
                                              — *Michel de Montaigne*

NINE-TENTHS of wisdom consists in being wise in time.
                                              — *Theodore Roosevelt*

WISDOM consists in conforming one's conduct both to reason and to feeling, to science as well as to faith, to the true as well as the beautiful.   — *Alexis Carrel*

WISDOM is of the soul.   — *Walt Whitman*

DAYS should speak, and multitude of years should teach wisdom.
                                              — *Job 32:7*

WE may be sure that if we can but find wisdom, all things else will be added unto us.   — *Will Durant*

WISDOM

BY three methods we may learn wisdom: First, by reflection, which is the noblest; Second, by imitation, which is the easiest; and third by experience, which is the bitterest. — *Confucius*

EVERY generation enjoys the use of a vast hoard of wisdom, bequeathed to it by antiquity, and transmits that hoard, augmented by fresh acquisitions, to future ages. — *Thomas B. Macaulay*

WISDOM is knowing what to do next; virtue is doing it.
— *D.S. Jordon*

WISDOM consists not as much in knowing what to do in the ultimate as in knowing what to do next. — *Herbert Hoover*

TO be mindful of my folly is already part of wisdom. — *Nikita Panin*

READING only fills the mind with Knowledge. Thinking and acting makes what we read ours. Wisdom is the proper use of Knowledge.
— *Alfred A. Montapert*

WISDOM is the principal thing, therefore get wisdom; and with all thy getting, get understanding. — *Proverbs 4:7*

WISE MAN

A TRULY wise man has both a keen interest in, and a definite respect for, the Laws of Nature. For these are the rules of life.
— *Alfred A. Montapert*

BE wiser than other people if you can, but do not tell them so.
— *Lord Chesterfield*

THE wise man has long ears and a short tongue. — *German Proverb*

WISE men learn more from fools than fools from the wise; for the wise avoid the error of fools, while fools do not profit by the examples of the wise. — *Cato*

A MAN is wise in proportion as he can judge facts in the light of principles, and thereby understand what he knows. — *Anonymous*

KNOWLEDGE is the treasure, but judgment the treasurer of a wise man. — *William Penn*

A WISE man will MAKE more opportunities than he finds. — *Sir Francis Bacon*

WISH

IF wishes were horses, beggars would ride. — *English Adage*

WATCH your wishes . . . be sure they're what you want . . . for wishes have a way of coming true. — *Mary Martin*

FEW things come to him who wishes; all things come to him who works. — *Anonymous*

HAPPY the man who early learns the wide chasm that lies between his wishes and his powers. — *Goethe*

WITNESS

GOD retained None of us as Lawyers, He called ALL of us as Witnesses! — *Dorothy B. White*

WOMAN

THE intuitions of woman are better and readier than those of men; her quick decisions without conscious reason are frequently far superior to a man's most careful deductions. — *W. Aikman*

WOMAN

THERE is a woman at the beginning of all great things.
— *Alphonse de Lamartine*

LOVE embraces woman's whole life; it is her prison and kingdom of heaven. — *Chamisso*

WHAT is truly indispensable for the conduct of life has been taught us by women . . . the small rules of courtesy, the actions that win us the warmth or deference of others; the words that assure us a welcome; the attitudes that must be varied to mesh with character or situation; all social strategy. It is listening to women that teaches us to speak to men. — *Remy de Gourmont*

ONCE made equal to man, woman becomes his superior. — *Socrates*

ALL women are perfection . . . especially she who loves you.
— *Alfred A. Montapert*

WORD OF GOD

THE crying need of the world today is a more intimate and thorough knowledge of the WORD OF GOD . . . With the WORD in your heart, YOU have PEACE and your load is lighter.
— *Frederick K. C. Price*

THOU hast the words of eternal life. — *John 6:68*

HEAVEN and earth shall pass away, but my words shall not pass away. — *Matthew 24:35*

WORDS

EATING words has never given me indigestion.
— *Sir Winston Churchill*

THE words of YOUR MOUTH can be YOUR FRIEND or YOUR ENEMY. You GET what you ORDER! — *Alfred A. Montapert*

AN honest man's word is as good as his bond.   — *Miguel de Cervantes*

WORDS are also seeds, and when dropped into the invisible spiritual substance, they grow and bring forth after their kind.
— Charles Fillmore

WORK

WORK is the grand cure for all the maladies and miseries that ever beset mankind, honest work, which you intend getting done.
— Thomas Carlyle

IT is the working man who is the happy man. It is the idle man who is the miserable man.   *— Benjamin Franklin*

WORK is the inevitable condition of human life, the true source of human welfare.   *— Leo Tolstoy*

WHAT the country needs is dirtier fingernails and cleaner minds.
— Will Rogers

BY the sweat of thy face shalt thou eat bread.   *— Genesis 3:19*

TEACH your boy to work and you will not need to leave him a fortune.   *— Roy L. Smith*

WORK is not man's punishment; it is his reward and his strength, his glory and his pleasure.   *— George Sand*

THE rule for every worthwhile man is that no serious job ever shall receive less than his best thought and effort.   *— William Feather*

BLESS thee in all the work of thy hand which thou doest.
— Deuteronomy 14:29

THE "Secret of Success" is no secret at all. It is the habit of hard work.   *— Anonymous*

WORK

"LEARN to like your work," is the first law of success and happiness in life. If you enjoy what you are doing, it is not work.   — *Councillor*

BY working faithfully eight hours a day, you may eventually get to be a boss and work twelve hours a day.   — *Robert Frost*

IT is easy to say NO. One need only sit and wait. In order to say YES, it is necessary to sweat and roll up one's sleeves, to seize life with both hands and plunge in up to one's elbows.   — *Jean Anouilh*

WORLD

REMEMBER thy prerogative is to govern, and not to serve, the things of the world.   — *Thomas a Kempis*

THE world is God's workshop for making men. — *Henry Ward Beecher*

THE riddle of the world is understood only by him who feels that God is good.   — *John Greenleaf Whittier*

WE LIVE IN TWO WORLDS. Everyone lives in the same outside Universe. Our outside world of space, stars, sun, moon, galaxies, woods, water and sky is wonderful. A Universe of Law and Order, a marvel of creation. HOWEVER, very few people realize they really live in a world that is inside of them. You create your own thoughts, beliefs, ideals and philosophy. From within, out of your Soul, proceedeth all Good and all Bad, for you live in your own inner world that YOU ALONE MAKE.   — *Alfred A. Montapert*

WORRY

THERE is nothing that wastes the body like worry, and one who has any faith in God should be ashamed to worry about anything whatsoever.   — *Mahatma Gandhi*

WHY worry, when you can pray.   *— Josephine R. Worth*

WORRY is unbelief; one cannot have faith and doubt. And worry is doubt. Worry never fixed anything, cured anything, or changed anything, only for the worse.   *— A. P. Gouthey*

IN just a few hours today will be yesterday . . . the tomorrow that you are worrying about. By worrying about tomorrow you try to live two days in one. That is impossible. Neither yesterday nor tomorrow can be made today. That is the reason why Jesus Christ erases all but today when He says, "Sufficient unto the day is the evil of today."
— Alfred A. Montapert

WORSHIP

WORSHIP is written upon the heart of many by the hand of God.
— Anonymous

AND what greater calamity can fall upon a nation than the loss of worship?   *— Ralph Waldo Emerson*

IT is only when men begin to worship that they begin to grow.
— Calvin Coolidge

WORTH

IF there is one rule for getting ahead, it is this: ALWAYS MAKE SURE YOU ARE UNDERPAID. It is far better to be worth more than you are paid, than to be paid more than you are worth. It sounds illogical, but the underpaid men make the most money.
— Elmer Wheeler

EVERYBODY is striving for what is not worth having.
— William M. Thackeray

NO man's private fortune can be an end any way worthy of his existence.   *— Sir Francis Bacon*

WORTH

FORGET not on every occasion to ask thyself, is this not one of the unnecessary things?
— Marcus Aurelius

WRITING

THE difficulty is not to write, but to write what you mean, not to affect your reader, but to affect him . . . precisely as you wish.
— Robert Louis Stevenson

THERE are three difficulties in authorship: to write anything worth the publishing, to find honest men to publish it, and to get sensible men to read it.
— Charles C. Colman

THE writer produces for the liberation of his soul. It is his nature to create, as it is the nature of water to run downhill.
— Anonymous

WRITE books like a telegram. Say a lot with a few well chosen words. Write in staccato sentences. Put in the QUALITY of material that uplifts the reader. Keep your writing simple, crystal clear, interesting and informative.
— Alfred A. Montapert

IF a man writes clearly enough, anyone can see if he fakes.
— Ernest Hemingway

MY aim is to put down on paper what I see and what I feel in the best and simplest way.
— Ernest Hemingway

IF you can think, then you can write.
— William Randolph Hearst

IF I weren't a violinist, I would like to be a writer. What would I write? A book on the shame and hypocrisy in our world. The kind of book few people would buy . . . about all the upside-down things in the world, the things that pretend to be one way, but aren't.
— Jascha Heifetz

IF a man writes a book, let him set down only what he knows. I have guesses enough of my own. — *Goethe*

BE SPECIFIC. What am I really trying to say? How well am I saying it? Am I conveying to the reader precisely what I wish? A careful writer must be a careful thinker. — *Alfred A. Montapert*

YEARNING

THE stomach is the only part of man which can be fully satisfied. The yearning of man's brain for new knowledge and experience and for more pleasant and comfortable surroundings never can be completely met. It is an appetite which cannot be appeased.

— *Thomas Alva Edison*

YOU/YOURSELF

THE environment YOU fashion out of . . . YOUR thoughts . . . YOUR beliefs . . . YOUR ideals . . . YOUR philosophy . . . is the only climate YOU will ever live in. — *Alfred A. Montapert*

EVERYONE is his own greatest enemy. — *Schefer*

GOD has delivered yourself to your care, and says, "I had no fitter to trust than you." — *Epictetus*

I DID not flee from men, but from affairs. We have lived long enough for others; let us live the rest for ourselves. Let us disentangle ourselves from the clutch of things which hold us elsewhere and keep us from ourselves. The greatest thing in the world is to know how to belong to yourself. — *Michel de Montaigne*

BE no one like another, yet every one like the Highest; do this and let each one be perfect in himself. — *Goethe*

YOU/YOURSELF

YOU owe no one as much as you owe yourself. You owe to yourself the action that opens for you the doors to the goodness, the variety, and the excitement of effort and success, of battle and victory. Making payment on this debt to yourself is the exact opposite of selfishness. You can best pay your debt to society, that has made you what you are, by being just yourself with all your might and as a matter of course . . . You fulfill the promise that lies latent within you by keeping your promises to yourself. — *David H. Fink*

YOUTH

YOUTH is not a time of life, it is a state of mind, it is a temper of the will, a quality of the imagination, a vigor of the emotions, a predominance of courage over timidity, of the appetite for adventure over love of ease. — *Unknown*

YOUTH is essentially of the spirit, not of the calendar. — *Anonymous*

YOUNG men are fitter to invent than to judge, fitter for execution than for counsel, and fitter for new projects than for settled business. — *Sir Francis Bacon*

THE years of youth, when there is less responsibility, are enjoyable . . . but the anxieties of youth are also very marked, and there are few young people who escape them. — *Eleanor Roosevelt*

ZEST

ZEST is the correlation of healthy mind and healthy body toward a healthy goal. It is the integrating character trait, an essential to life and happiness. — *W. Beran Wolfe*

LET us put more LIFE into our LIVING. — *Alfred A. Montapert*